MW00927740

"As a Psychotherapist, I often hear men and women talk about how challenging dating can be because they don't understand why the opposite sex acts the way they do. Lisa did a great job of translating the subtle (and not so subtle) cues, which men put out for women. *The Winning Dating Formula For Women Over 50* offers practical tips ranging from how to create a winning online profile to why men might not be calling for a second date. After reading Lisa's book I fine-tuned some of the things I was unconsciously doing on dates and I have to say, I'm quite pleased with the results!" - Lisa Stromeier, *LISW, Founder and Chef Choice Innovator at Creating Choices for Health*

"Lisa's insights and experience into understanding what men really want are more than just another 'self-help' guide. By taking a good look at what you truly want and don't want, the door opens to finding a quality man through self discovery. I think Lisa guides the reader and her coaching clients to discover their innate magnificence that results in making dating fun." - Fred Wright, Singles Tour Operator, **www.enchantedislandtravels.com**

"Lisa has the ability to change dating despair into dating hope for women over 50. She takes the dating process to a high level of self-awareness and self-growth. Once she helps you identify who your are and what you want, dreams can come true." - Sarah Weiss, Medical Intuitive, Spirithealonline.com

"As a woman over 50, you decide to venture back into the

dating world and find it a bit scary, yet exciting! Not sure what to do or how to begin? Let Lisa Copeland take you by the hand and guide you to successful dating. Lisa's book, *The Winning Dating Formula For Women Over 50*, is filled with valuable, down-to-earth information and her personal experiences of how to "get out there" and have fun dating quality men. Your confidence and natural beauty will shine as you put into practice the 7 Steps. Whether you are just starting out or have been dating for a while, this is a must read for all women over 50 who desire to find a quality man." - Gretchen M. Fox, Author of *Raising A Child's Awareness: An Educator's Guide to Happier, Empowered Children*, Certified Life Coach, Cincinnati, OH

"Lisa does a fantastic job of capturing the difficulties we strong women have when trying to find a man. I really appreciate how she highlights our qualities and encourages us to move out of our comfort zone in step three. It's hard to produce different results when you do the same things over and over. Thanks Lisa!" - Jennifer Diepstraten, **www.familyco.com**

"Lisa is so helpful in sorting through the steps to find what you really want in your man. I loved her Top 20 Dating Strategies for Finding Mr. Right - especially #19, have a dating strategy in place. And now I do, thanks to this book!" -Mary Young, Phoenix, AZ

"Lisa's book is very helpful! Thanks for making this information available. I recommend this for anyone over 50 who is looking, whether divorced, widowed, or never married." - Dannis Cole

"I can't believe how helpful and simple Step 5 was about where to find quality men and how to approach a man you find interesting! Sometimes it's the most obvious places that we take for granted. Great suggestion to check out men in the grocery store! After reading Lisa's book, I actually asked a man about something that he was buying. I gave him the '5 second look' first! Thanks, Lisa for reminding me about the little things in life that are easy and important!" – Marlene, Chicago

"Lisa has hit this 'out of the park' with her new book *The Winning Dating Formula For Women Over 50*. Dating is never easy anyway, but for so many women who have found a comfort zone within a family structure for so many years, to be literally catapulted onto the dating scene again, dating is nothing short of terrifying. Lisa has literally left no stone unturned in what a woman over 50 needs to know about dating, relationships in today's world and what it takes to find magic the second or even third time around. *The Winning Dating Formula For Women Over 50* is a step by step by step guide that will take you by the hand and guide you toward not only a successful dating life, but creating the best opportunity for you to find 'Mr. Wonderful' by creating change from the inside out if you follow her advice and years of first-hand experience in this area. I not only highly recommend Lisa's book, but recommend Lisa's coaching for any woman who truly desires to fall in love for the last time in her life." - Susan Turnbull, Transformational Beliefs Coach and Host of *Breakthrough!* on Positive Living Vibrations Radio

You are invited to receive my free report...
5 Little Known Secrets To Finding A Quality Man!
Visit my website at **http://www.FindAQualityMan.com**
to download your copy today.

To your dating success!

Lisa

The Winning Dating Formula
For Women Over 50

7 Steps To Attracting Quality Men

By Lisa Copeland

www.FindAQualityMan.com

This book is designed to provide information that the author believes to be accurate on the subject matter it covers, but it is sold with the understanding that neither the author nor the publisher is offering individualized advice tailored to any specific dating situation.

Past results do not guarantee future results. No warranty is made with respect to the accuracy or completeness of the information contained herein, and both the author and the publisher specifically disclaim any responsibility for any liability, loss, or risk, personal or otherwise which is incurred as a consequence, directly or any liability, loss or risk, personal or otherwise, which is incurred as a consequence, directly or indirectly of the use and application of any of the contents of this book.

In the text that follows, many people's names and identifying characteristics have been changed. This information should not be used as a substitute for help from a licensed professional.

First Printing, 2013
Second Printing 2015

Find A Quality Man
8345 NW 66th St. Suite 4215
Miami, Florida 33166

For more information, please contact us at **www.FindAQualityMan.com**

ISBN 978-1492746263

Dedicated to the strong, single women over 50 who are committed to doing what it takes to find love again.

CONTENTS

Step 4... Getting A Clear Vision Of The Man You Want In Your Life

Step 5... Your Dating Blueprint

Step 6... Online Dating

Step 7... The Etiquette Of Dating After 50

An Introduction To The Winning Dating Formula...

It's assumed we should know what to do when it comes to dating. This is not true! I can't begin to tell you how many women share with me the dread and fear they feel thinking about dating at this time in their lives.

Women successful in other areas of their lives are plagued with low self-esteem from marriages where compliments ended years ago. Some women have come from a good marriage but a spouse passed away and no man is living up to the past. Other women are just beginning to date and aren't sure how to go about the process of dating.

Women tell me stories of being single for 20 plus years with no interest in dating until now. Some women are just starting on their dating journey and like women who haven't dated in years don't know where to begin. Some women are in dating ruts and can't seem to shift out of the mindset of "there's no one out there to date."

You're in the right place if you identify with any of these scenarios.

I've been right there with you. When my first marriage ended in my mid 40's, I was clueless how to get out there and date. I made so many mistakes... Posting pictures online with my dad, letting men choose me, flying off to Australia to meet a guy and the list goes on.

"Failure is only postponed success." ~Herbert Kaufman

Unfortunately, since no on handed me a dating rulebook with my divorce papers, I found myself constantly frustrated and often crushed by dating at this age. I didn't understand why men would say and do the things they did.

I didn't understand how to get a man to notice me and I didn't know how to flirt with one if he did. It had been years since I'd flirted and my skills were beyond RUSTY.

I did end up in relationships with men but not the types of men I really wanted. Why? Because no one ever told me to get a **clear vision** of who I wanted to be with.

Oh, I made lists of qualities, but some I didn't feel worthy of having, and it's so true when they say that the universe brings you exactly what you want and feel worthy of having in life.

I ended up in a second marriage based on the type of chemistry that leads to the *hottest* sex ever. It was great until my mom got sick and nearly died. With no friendship in place – and how could there be when all we were good at was hanging out in bed all day – our relationship fell apart.

That's when I went hunting for help. But no one was out there to guide me as a single 50-year-old woman fresh out of a second marriage. Oh, there were coaches out there but they were young... as in my kid's age. I couldn't imagine telling them my fears about being over 50 and dating. There was no way they could relate.

So I began researching and learning everything I could about dating and men. I figured out the tools and skills that worked for women our age and I began dating Quality Men.

I began teaching these same tools and skills to my friends who were also over 50. What happened? They started having fun dating too! That's when I realized there were probably other women my age that could use these same tools I'd uncovered.

I started coaching what I'd discovered to as many women as I could. I helped them see how awesome they are as women and how wonderful men really are once you understand them. It's all in the seven steps you're about to learn in the Winning Dating Formula for having fun while finding love after 50.

I've been in the dating trenches. Dating is tough at our age. So many women quit when it gets hard because they just don't know how to handle the ups and downs that continuously pop up.

They end up alone and unhappy. I don't want you be one of those statistics and that's why I wrote this book… to give you the information you need after 50 to have fun dating as you look for love with that special man.

This book is for you if you're just beginning to date or you've been dating but have found it so frustrating you're on the verge of quitting. I did all the heavy lifting and made all the crazy and dumb mistakes so you won't have to.

And I've put the information I've learned and researched into 7 easy steps that are geared for single women over 50. Whether you're divorced, widowed or even if you've never married, this information can help you.

I want to help you make your dream of finding a Quality Man come true. This book is a great start and I congratulate you for having the courage to take this step. I've learned the only way for making your dreams come true is by taking action and that's what you're doing by being here!

If you find you'd like to go deeper with these steps, I'd love to be your Dating Coach, mentoring you over the humps that will occur… the fears that will try and hold you back and the triumph you will feel as you meet the guy you've dreamed of.

Nothing gives me greater joy than helping women make

their dreams come true. If you find you'd like personal help with your dating situation, drop me a note at **Lisa@findaqualityman.com** and we'll find a time to chat about how I can personally help you find and meet your Mr. Right.

Lisa

"The Perfect Guy is not the one who has the most money or is the most handsome one you'll meet.
He's the one who knows how to make you smile and will take care of you each and every day until the end of time."
~Author Unknown

LISA COPELAND

Step 1... From Insecure To Dating With Confidence

Understanding What Makes You Desirable And Attractive To Quality Men

You're Single For The First Time In A Long Time...Now What?

"Until you get comfortable with being alone, you'll never know if you're choosing someone out of love or loneliness."

~Author Unknown

To this day, I can remember my very first night alone after my 24-year marriage ended. It was scary taking off my wedding ring for the last time getting into bed knowing I was alone and single for the first time in over two decades.

At the same time, I felt this sense of freedom and exhilaration. This was an opportunity to get to know me again.

I no longer had to fight over the TV remote. These were the days before DVR'S, so I was finally able to watch an entire show without channel surfing through every commercial.

Being in control of the TV remote became a symbol of gaining control over my life and it felt great!

---

into a single closet where nothing could be found and

everything got wrinkled. I now had a winter and summer closet and I loved it!

If I didn't feel like cooking, I didn't have to. And for sure, I didn't have to go to the trouble of making a time-consuming meal only to hear: "I had that for lunch." Now, I could eat anytime I wanted and have any type of food I wanted.

I changed a few things in my home and made it feel more like *me*. It felt cozy and comfortable and I loved coming home so I could sink into my favorite chair to read a book or call a friend.

I began to find my own style and found I no longer needed anyone else's approval or agreement to implement it.

But single and living on your own for the first time in a long time can feel pretty uncomfortable at times. Sitting alone staring at the four walls... you realize you've forgotten what it is YOU love in life.

For years, you were probably bending like a pretzel compromising yourself to meet someone else's wishes and demands. Often what you wanted came second.

Now you get to come first! The gift in all of this is you have the opportunity to discover who YOU are again. It's exciting and yet at the same time – I know and understand – you can feel so alone.

"You are the finest, lovelies, tenderest, and most beautiful person I have ever known-and even that is an understatement."
~F. Scott Fitzgerald

Coping With Loneliness

Being alone night after night can feel both scary and isolating as you eat dinner and watch TV with no one to talk to. Your first thoughts may be to run out and find a man to fill the void you're feeling in your life.

I urge you not to. Instead, take some time to heal your wounds and get to know yourself again.

You see, as women, we think we need a man to complete us in life. It's far healthier when a man compliments you rather than completes you. For a man to do this, you'll want to discover who you are again. And you'll want to let go of who your ex thought you were while you were married.

Forgetting who you are and what you love in your life is what's caused you to feel so lonely.

When you start dating too soon after a breakup, you are giving up this important step of finding YOU again. What happens is you end up bringing what you didn't heal in your last relationship right back into your life with a new man and a new relationship. This is your BAGGAGE.

"It is only the first step that is difficult."

~Marie De Vichy-Chamrond

Get back in touch with yourself by going online looking for activities and classes that feel like fun for you. Chances are you stopped doing the activities you loved a long time ago. Pick one up again or find new activities you might enjoy.

You're single now, but it doesn't mean you have to be alone every weekend. Ask your friends if they have girlfriends who are also single so you have someone to go to a movie or out to dinner with.

Fulfilled by doing the things you love doing and being with the people you love being with... you'll start to sparkle with an inner glow. You'll get compliments from friends thinking you cut your hair or lost weight. But you'll know where it really comes from. It's an inner confidence from getting to know you again. This is when you are your most exciting and enticing to men.

Your Inner Glow is the number one quality men will be so attracted to in you!

Why Dating After 50 Feels So Scary

"No matter how attractive a person's potential may be, you have to date their reality." ~Mandy Hale

As a Dating Coach, I've witnessed so many women over 50 literally stop themselves from dating by allowing fear and self doubt to keep them out of the dating game.

They are playing it safe and often, they're not even aware of it. Here's what I mean...women say they are lonely and they want a man in their life, and they'd do anything to find him.

But when push comes to shove, it becomes a totally different story. For many women, when it's time to date again, they're uncertain of the steps they need to take for doing the work that results in finding Quality Men to date.

In many ways, it's a lot easier to go out with friends or stay home every Saturday night, complaining "no good men are really out there anyway" than it is to date.

Does this story sound familiar to you?

It's actually the inner self-doubt and fear you're experiencing that is keeping you from getting back out in the real dating world. So you end up using excuses like... "I don't have time now," "I'm too busy," or "I'm traveling to see my grandchildren." I understand.

Nothing feels worse than rejection from a man you'd like to date.

Yet to find the special man you've been wanting, you have to be willing to step out of your comfort zone and date. Some men will like you, and some won't. Some men you'll like, and some you won't. But unless you try dating lots of different types of men, you'll never know who the right one is for you.

Getting the relationship you desire means facing your fears and walking through them even when it feels scary and uncomfortable. Caving in to your fears means not being able to get what it is you want in life.

Dating after such a long time is scary. You may feel like

you're not thin enough, pretty enough, or interesting enough to attract a man.

It's so important to take time after a relationship to regroup and find the real you again. You are perfect as you are and you will want to find a Quality Man who sees you that way as well.

What's going to help you overcome your fears is shifting your mindset to one of viewing a date as an opportunity to meet a new and interesting man. That's it! If you like the guy and he likes you, great!

If it doesn't work out, there are plenty of other men to date whether online, in real life or through your *Dating Fairy Godmothers*. You'll learn more about exactly who they are and how they can help you find Quality Men to date later in this book. Miracles start to happen when you give as much energy to your dreams as you do to your fears.

"Real LOVE is an expresion of internal productivity and includes caring, respect, responsibility and knowledge."
~Author Unknown

To sum it up, don't rush into dating after your marriage or a new relationship has ended. Allow yourself to enjoy this time of getting to know you again. It is a gift only you can give yourself.

Leaving Your Baggage In The Past
"Tell the negative committee that meets inside your head to sit down and shut up." ~Ann Bradford

Everyone comes with baggage. Yet doesn't it feel, as you've gotten older like you've accumulated a lot more of it? When you were young and getting married for the first time, you came with very little baggage.

It's likely whatever you had probably fit into a small carrying case that included a couple of high school and college sweethearts along with whatever issues you might have had with your parents.

Let's move forward 20 years. If you're reading this book, it's likely you've experienced the loss of a spouse either through passing or divorce. Your small case has grown into a steam trunk filled with children, grandchildren, aging parents, in-laws from your past, friends, houses, and debt just to name a few.

And all of these get carried into your next relationship.

Men will have baggage too. The key is being able to let go of the baggage you no longer need, then integrate what's left into your new relationship.

It starts with talking openly about what you're both carrying into the relationship. It's harder to compromise as we get older. The baggage you both bring isn't going to go away. And as much as you may want to change it, you won't be able to. So it's important for you to take a good look at what you can and can't live with.

Will Men Want To Date Me At My Age?
"The Sexiest curve on your body is your smile. Flaunt it."
~Growingbolder.com

The answer is a definite YES! As a woman over 50, you're going to be amazed at how many men will be interested in you! You'll have younger ones looking for a cougar, men your age who want to share a common history with you and older men who will feel younger just imagining you at their side.

It's exciting! And the cool thing about men is they want nothing more than to please you and make you happy. Yes, you read that right.

The key is appreciating their efforts every single time they do something for you.

Are You Ready To Date?

"There comes a time in your life, when you walk away from all the drama and people who create it.
You surround yourself with people who make you laugh.
Forget the bad, and FOCUS ON THE GOOD.
Love the people who treat you right,
Pray for the ones who don't.
Life is too short to be
ANYTHING BUT HAPPY.
Fall down is part of life,
Getting back up is living".
~Jose N. Harris

You can gauge your readiness by asking yourself this simple

question…when you picture your ex, how do you feel? If he can still invoke strong feelings of anger, you might want to think about taking a little more time to heal before you begin dating.

When you don't take the time to finish healing, what happens is you end up going on a date with a new guy talking and processing about the old guy… the good, the bad and the ugly. Men dislike when this happens. Think how you feel when all they do is talk about how horrid their ex's are.

When you bash your ex, men will label you a "Drama Queen." And if you've had the opportunity to read men's profiles, you'll know how many men say please don't contact me if this is you.

Use this healing time to figure out why the last relationship didn't work so you don't end up dragging your unfinished baggage into the new relationship. To prove this point, take a look at the men your friends choose to date over and over again.

How many times have you thought, *she's dating a guy who looks and acts just like her ex?*

The second question to ask yourself is… How would you rate your **dating confidence** on a scale from one to ten with ten being the highest?

Ending a relationship can be brutal. Ex's can say things that make you doubt yourself and cause you to forget just how AWESOME you really are. In the next chapter, we'll talk more about how to develop your Dating Confidence so you feel wonderful when you get out there and start dating new men.

Know that loving yourself totally and completely sends vibes into the world of a happy, confident and openhearted woman who's ready to attract a great guy!

When you feel good about you, you'll get your dating mojo back a lot quicker. Another benefit – your mojo is what creates an inner and outer glow in you that man are so unbelievably attracted to!

The last question to ask yourself is… are you ready to flirt and have fun dating at this time in your life? When you think about it, how long has it been since you last flirted?

It's probably been quite a while! Yet it's the best tool you have for getting a great guy to notice you whether it's online or in the real world. And it's going to mean getting comfortable with feeling uncomfortable. Flirting again over 50 can feel strange.

But as we'll talk about throughout this book, it's your main signal for letting a guy know you're interested in him! So get out there and start talking and laughing with every man around you, whether he's single or married.

You know what they say…
PRACTICE MAKES PERFECT!

Lighting Your Inner Fire That Men Love!

"Happiness is when you feel good about yourself without feeling the need for anyone else's approval." ~Author Unknown

Do you sometimes find yourself having a difficult time

accepting yourself as the wonderful woman you really are? When you look in the mirror, do you see your magnificence or does every flaw pop out and drive you crazy?

Maybe you've gained a few pounds over the years or gravity and wrinkles are taking their toll. You just aren't feeling good enough to be a player in the dating game so you put off dating using excuses like *no good man would want me this way* or *I have to lose ten pounds before I can go online.*

"I think happiness is what makes you pretty. Period! Happy people are beautiful. They become like a mirror and they reflect that happiness." ~Drew Barrymore

This happens to all of us. Here's how you can get out of this funk. I want you to make a list of 10 to 20 qualities YOU love about your body, your personality and what you love to do or are good at.

Lets face it, we're over 50 and some of our body parts just aren't as tight and firm as they used to be when we were in our 20's and 30's.

I want you to remember that a man didn't know you in your 20's and 30's. He's attracted to the beautiful women he sees RIGHT NOW either in person or online.

He doesn't know your arms didn't jiggle back then and in all honesty, even though you see it every time you look in the mirror, it's not something he's focused on.

We're going to put in place a new mindset about the parts of your body that you are having a hard time loving. Instead, think of how grateful you feel that you have those jiggling arms because you can use them to hug all the people you love in your life.

Moving from a negative focus to a gratitude focus can change how you feel about your body. It will help you see

how amazing your body really is!

Everyday, look in the mirror and read at least one of your lists out loud to the beautiful woman looking back at you. This is a very powerful exercise that will help you feel good about yourself, thus rebuilding your Dating Confidence.

I can remember being at the grocery store. I reached into the dairy section to pick up a container of yogurt. On the sides of most dairy cases are mirror and I remember seeing my reflection smiling at me and I looked back at her and thought, *I really like you!*

This is where I want you to be. Instead of looking in the mirror seeing all your negative qualities, I want you to really see the magnificent woman you are.

To make this happen requires committing to reminding yourself daily of your magnificence using the lists you're going to make.

There are going to be times when you'll forget how awesome you are and you'll backslide. It may happen when you go bathing suit shopping or when you're looking for a dress as the mother of the bride or groom.

Looking at yourself in the mirror, all you can see are the lumps, bumps and wrinkles on your body. And it's likely you'll find yourself heading in a downward spiral of thinking negatively about your body again.

This is the time you'll want to play what I like to call the **"3 to 1 Game."** For every negative thought you tell yourself, you'll want to grab your lists and remind yourself of three positive qualities you love about you. This is how you'll make huge changes in your Dating Confidence Mindset.

The "3 to 1 Game" is also a great game to play with future men in your life when something about them is bugging you. It will help you get back in touch with why you were attracted to this man in the first place.

Your goal is to become conscious of how much you have

been beating yourself up. Then to STOP IT! We all have flaws. When you focus on your flaws, they become far bigger in your minds than the good qualities you are forgetting to see.

"Your worth does not revolve around what others think. Your worth is what you put in yourself and know in your heart."
~Author Unknown

It's time to love and accept the whole you. I'll tell you right now... Men don't look at your pieces and parts the way you do. They decide whether they'd like to date you based on the whole you that you present.

When you feel good about who you are as a beautiful woman over 50, you will glow. This is the number one quality for attracting the Quality Men you'd like to date.

What Fun... A Dating Makeover!

"You are about to meet someone that loves you in a way you deserve to be loved." ~Chinese fortune cookie

Let's enhance your dating confidence and inner glow with some dating updating. If you've been in a long marriage, there's a good chance your dressing like a suburban housewife in the most comfortable clothes you own; not exactly what's going to make you feel desirable when you head out on a date with the man you really want in your life.

A couple of simple dating updates can take you from

feeling dowdy and outdated to feeling chic, confident and pretty spectacular.

It's an investment in yourself as you begin this next exciting chapter in your life!

So where do you start? If you have a daughter or a close friend who will be truthful yet kind, confide in them what you're doing and ask them to give you an honest opinion on what about your overall look could use some updating.

I have found daughters love this job. When I first started dating in my 40's, I can remember my daughter saying, "Mom, you have to get rid of those granny panties!"

They were so comfortable but I have to admit she was right! I did change them and in doing so felt far sexier than I did in the grannies. And although I never thought I'd get used to the hip cut, I did and now I'd never go back.

Our adult children have this innate sense of style we missed growing up during a time when dressing like a hippie was the fashion standard.

Remember what you wore as a teenager? My uniform was torn jeans (the funny thing is...now you pay a lot for those tears that are considered *stylish* in the eyes of current designers), my dad's Army jacket, my grandma's black seal coat and black converse tennis shoes, which by the way, are back in style too.

Now, fast-forward 25 years and it's no wonder I had no sense of style! It took getting some help from my daughter and professionals to get myself looking dateable again.

*"Most people are searching for happiness outside themselves.
That's a fundamental mistake. Happiness is something you are,
and it comes from the way you think about you."*
~Author Unknown

Starting from the top, work down your body as you figure out exactly what you'd like to do about creating a new dating look.

Start by taking a look at your hairstyle. It's pretty easy to get into a rut here and I'll share with you an example. A friend and I have tickets for the Broadway plays that come to our area. For years, we've sat next to a woman who still sports a 1970's Dorothy Hamill wedge. She's in her 60's still wearing a 'do that hasn't been updated in 40 years.

There's a big difference between a timeless classic hairstyle and an outdated hairstyle. One can actually make look older than you really are.

This is a good time to reevaluate hair color. You want a stylist who will use the right colors to enhance your skin tone. At our age, hair that's too dark makes us look rather *gothic* while too light might fade us out.

Next, treat yourself and visit a good makeup counter at a department store near you. The women behind those counters are trained makeup artists who can introduce you to some great colors that will enhance your features. You can always replicate the results with less expensive makeup purchased elsewhere if you want.

Beware! You're used to viewing yourself in the mirror with specific styles and colors you're comfortable with. Change can feel awkward at first. You may think a new color is awful when in fact, it actually looks great on you. Sometimes, it just takes getting used to.

"We Were Given Two Hands To Hold,
Two Legs To Walk,
Two Eyes To See,
Two Ears To Listen,
But Why Only One Heart?
Because the other one was given to someone for us to find."
~Unknown Author

This is why it helps to take a trusted friend with you. Your friend isn't attached to your old look. She can be more objective about the new color, hairstyle or outfit and will be able to give you an honest opinion on whether or not a new look is working for you.

Do give yourself some time to get used to the changes you're making.

Now let's move to clothes. Shopping can be fun, if you're into it. I'm not a shopper and that is why the second I found out about department store **personal shoppers**, I was thrilled. And what's so great is most larger department stores don't charge you for this service. They make their money on what you buy.

Clothing is an area where you can get stuck... Do you find yourself wearing the same look over and over again just in different colors? Be honest – how many of the same tops did you buy in different colors because it looked pretty good on you?

What I love about going to a personal shopper is... she gently pushes me into trying new styles that actually enhance the best parts of my body. I started getting compliments that only confirmed how much better I was beginning to feel about myself both inside and out as the result of the changes I was making.

Another benefit – for the first time in my life, I felt really good in what I was wearing. I no longer rummaged through my closet looking for something that felt just right for a date. Knowing I always had a couple of nice pieces I could easily mix and match at a moment's notice made a huge difference in my confidence levels.

All of that said, you don't have to use a personal shopper and you don't have to shop at expensive stores to look and feel great. Browse fashion magazines or check out the style shows on TV for great ideas and tips on how to best enhance your body with clothes.

Looking great makes you feel great. When you feel great, you are going to feel confident as you venture into the dating world. This type of confidence is very attractive to men!

Step 2... Getting In Touch With The Feminine Woman Inside You

Your Femininity Is The Secret To Dating Quality Men Who Make You Feel Safe, Protected, Loved And Cherished

Discovering The Sometimes Forgotten Female Inside Of You

"Our days are happier when we give people a piece of our heart rather than a piece of our mind." ~Author Unknown

Growing up in the 60's and 70's, we were indoctrinated with mantras like… *Burn your bra… You never need a man…* or *You can do it as well or better than he can.*

Women's Lib made great strides in opening career doors that had previously been closed to women. But when it came to finding love, it has played havoc in the Dating and Relationship Game. No one is quite sure of the roles they are supposed to be playing anymore.

Women forgot how to be in touch with the qualities men really want and that's their softer side and their emotional side.

Women having had to make powerful decisions on a daily basis, became Alpha Females and ended up finding themselves competing with men in their love and career lives.

Dr. Pat Allen, a psychologist who has spent her life discovering how deeply relationships are affected by these roles, believes it doesn't matter who the Alpha is and who's the Beta is as long as there is only one of each in the relationship.

In today's dating world there are four different combinations of Alpha and Beta that can show up on a date.

1. An Alpha Female and an Alpha Male
2. An Alpha Male and a Beta Female
3. An Alpha Female and a Beta Male
4. A Beta Female and a Beta Male

How do you know whether you're an Alpha or a Beta Female? You'll want to start by asking yourself this question... Which quality is **more important** to you – being cherished or being respected by a man? Both are in every relationship but one is always more dominate.

If you said respected first, it's likely you are an Alpha Female, who uses masculine energy in her love relationships.

See if you can identify with some of these Alpha characteristics...
- **You like being in control of the situation.**
- **You want to be the MAIN decision maker.**
- **You can be bossy.**
- **You're competitive.**
- **You can be critical.**
- **You can be very analytical.**

- You may say it sweetly but you're still being demanding or competitive.
- You offer opinions to a man about how things should be whether or not he's asked for your thoughts.
- You are a huge GIVER... maybe even an OVERGIVER.

If on the other hand, you found yourself saying you'd love to be cherished first, it's likely you're a Beta Female who uses powerful feminine energy with a man.

Some of the characteristics of a Beta Female are...

- You allow a man to give to you.
- You recognize your feminine power and use it.
- You listen to a man, offering him support, yet you don't offer an opinion until you are asked for one.
- You come from a place of vulnerability and a willingness to let a man help you out.
- You receive from a man.

As a feminine woman, you'll want to know how to receive from men. Men truly want to give to you in the best way they can. Why? Because it plays, again, into their role of wanting to keep you safe, protected and provided for.

"Love comes to those who still hope even though they've been disappointed, to those who still believe even though they've been betrayed, to those who still love even though they've been hurt before." ~Author Unknown

If you come from your true feminine power, you are going to be able to get what you need and want from a man without giving up any part of yourself like we do when we nag men. Nagging turns men off. It doesn't allow them to step up and be your hero.

I want you to think of Scarlett O'Hara in *Gone With The Wind*, sitting under a huge tree surrounded by men wanting nothing more than to please her. They loved her because she made every single one of them feel special and needed by her. Remember all the barbeque they fetched for her? They couldn't do enough for her.

In today's world, you can have men doing this for you as well. You just have to stop putting yourself in the position of competing with a man. You can start by asking a man for his help. Even something as simple as letting him open a jar for you makes him feel needed and wanted by you.

How do you do this? Women have a tendency to ask men for help the same they would ask another woman for help. You might say something like, "Can you help me move this table?" Women are fine hearing it asked this way but men hear a statement like this as demanding.

If you want a man to help you with something, consider using these four magic words, "I need your help," then watch how this changes your life with men.

Men over 50 want nothing more than to make you happy. They will give to you in every way possible as long as it's within their power to do so. The problem is a man might not do it the way you want it done.

You criticize the job he's done because you think it should have been done differently. He perceives you as coming across as controlling and he thinks you've emasculated him by not allowing him to be a man.

I want to share a story with you about how coming into your true feminine power can work for you with men in all areas of your life.

Elizabeth, a client of mine, is a powerhouse at work. She knows how to get the job done quickly and efficiently. At work, she's a true Alpha Female. And her Alpha characteristics were also showing up in her dating life, sending men running to the hills as fast as they could go.

Elizabeth wasn't ready to practice her feminine skills just yet in a dating situation. So she decided to try them out at work with men, figuring it was where she felt most comfortable.

She had a meeting scheduled with the CEO of a major corporation. In the past, she'd have come into the meeting much like a bull in a china shop would have. She'd have pushed and forced issues until the deal was signed, sealed and delivered.

This time, Elizabeth decided to take a more feminine approach. She consciously made a decision to wear softer feminine clothing versus the usual black suit which screams an ALPHA FEMALE is approaching.

If you dress in a black suit, consider dressing it up with a feminine tank and softer jewelry to make you appear less masculine and aggressive to men.

Elizabeth slowed herself down as she went into the meeting and told the very macho CEO the four magic words men love to hear... "I need your help."

He gladly stepped up and within five minutes the deal was sealed. They spent the next hour talking. He shared a lot about his life, which is a man's way of trying to impress you and by the end of the conversation, he told her to call on him anytime she needed his help.

She was astonished by this "miracle" of how easy it was to get a man's cooperation once she knew how to do it.

In the past...coming from her masculine Alpha side, it had taken a lot of struggle and head butting, plus hours versus minutes to get the deal sealed; that is if it got sealed at all.

So why do I tell you this story? Before Elizabeth started working with me...she only knew how to come from her masculine Alpha Side and she was turning men off right and left in both business and in love.

She found that by asking a man to step up and help her, she witnessed what every woman witnesses when she consciously flips the switch to her feminine side, men stepping over themselves to help her.

Using your feminine side, men feel like you really get who they are and that you understand them. In dating, they'll want to connect with you on the emotional level they crave with a woman. This is the true power of the feminine mystique.

Why Alpha Females Have a Hard Time Catching An Alpha Male

"Benefits of dating me: You will be dating me. I could go on but I think I have made my point." ~someecards

If you are an Alpha Female, you have worked hard to move up the corporate ladder or get to where you are today professionally. You're the leader who's making important decisions all day long.

Then you come home and you're expected to just shut it off and become a kitten or a Beta Female to your big, strong Alpha male. Quite honestly, it's pretty hard to do.

After 15 years of being single, Jan, a CEO of a large company decided she was ready for a relationship that could lead to marriage. She, like so many women over 50, is a dynamic, powerhouse women.

Jan looks great as so many women our age do. She's leading a successful life, and just as your friends say to you, Jan is told over and over again how she's such a great catch.

And she is. She's been a role model for women in her field for many years. She has a great sense of style, her friends and associates admire her and she has a large network of friends, both male and female.

So what is happening here? Why can't Jan, and other powerful women of our generation, find a man to marry? Powerful women like Jan usually want to date a man who's just like she is… smart, successful, and respected!

Often what women like Jan don't understand is the Alpha Man to whom she's most attracted does not want to get involved with a woman who is a clone of himself. More than likely, this man is looking for a woman who will allow him to be a man and who will appreciate what he does for her.

Women of our generation were rarely advised on how to receive from a man. If anything, we were taught we didn't need men in our lives. We were encouraged to become strong and independent and we learned to take care of ourselves with or without a man's presence around us.

We've spent years fighting our way to the top of the corporate ladder becoming successful, powerful and influential women in our fields. We are used to making decisions and we know how to get things done.

We are the president at work and we want to be the president at home. We don't know how to turn those feeling off when it comes to men. Yet what we want in our lives is often an Alpha Male, a male who will make us feel loved, cherished and protected.

When we don't allow an Alpha Male to play his role, we are threatening an ingrained DNA role from caveman days of him needing to be the provider. An Alpha Man looks at women like Jan and doesn't know how to play the provider role of being able to give to Jan in a way that will make her happy.

In his eyes, she doesn't need him. Men this age need to be needed or they move on, often times seeking the companionship of a younger woman who does.

It's not necessarily the eye candy he's looking for but the appreciation and the hero status he craves. And that's what these younger women give to him by joyfully receiving his gifts. Something women our age don't always do.

An Alpha Man wants to cherish his woman by showing her he can protect her financially, emotionally and physically to the best of his ability. This role makes a woman like Jan feel safe and protected. In theory, she likes his decisiveness. In reality, she often has a hard time letting him be the leader.

The Alpha Man might love her body and her mind but will quickly tire of competing with her for the leadership role. A Beta Male is a better fit for Jan and other powerful women out there. These men will respect her and let her make the major decisions in the relationship.

In return, she will cherish him. Don't get confused thinking he's a wimp for letting her be the leader. He will just have other qualities to offer the relationship like the ability to emotionally support Jan in a way an Alpha Man can't.

Wouldn't it be nice to have a man who wants to nurture you after a hard day at work? Like an Alpha Male, Jan will get to be the president in both the boardroom and at home.

"Success isn't just what you accomplish in life, it's about what you inspire others to do and be." ~Author Unknown

If this is you too, you just might find by choosing a Beta Male, you have a man in your life who loves and adores you just the way you are as a dynamic, powerful successful woman.

Why Doing It All Gets You Nowhere Fast!

"Some changes look negative on the surface but you will soon realize that space is being created in your life for something new to emerge." ~Eckhart Tolle

I want to fill you in on a secret. It wasn't long ago that I was a major Alpha Female. Not only did I know how to do it all,

I held the belief I could do it even better and faster than most men. I felt powerful and I loved that power.

The problem was what I was feeling was my Masculine Power not my Feminine Power and I ended up being told by different men that I was controlling, emasculating and even worse, (these words that shocked me) I didn't know how to let a man be a man. And in all honesty, when I look back, I can see I didn't.

I wasn't taught the power of my feminine nature or how to get my needs met in a relationship with a man or truthfully, how to be a partner. I just wanted to be in control.

Growing up, I learned how to become a powerhouse who stepped on men regardless of their feelings or how my behavior made them feel. And what I found out was this brings out the WORST in a man.

The men who accused me of not letting them be men couldn't tell me in words what made them feel emasculated or less than as a man.

But I was on a mission to find out what this meant. I began researching men and how they lived their lives. I found out what makes them tick. I'll tell you that being an Alpha Female for sure doesn't do it.

When we were in high school, rumor had it that we had to be dumber than a man for him to like us. Not true! A man wants a woman in his life who is intelligent and can think for herself.

He's wants a woman at his side who can support him as he will for her on their journey together. He respects a woman who knows what she wants. It's how she presents it that often gets her in trouble.

So what do I mean by this? Men absolutely, positively don't want to be controlled or told what to do or how to do it. When you tell a guy how to do his job at home or at work, especially when he hasn't asked for your opinion, he feels less than or inadequate in your eyes. He feels like nothing he does will every make you happy.

All a man wants to do is be your hero and he tries his very best to be that for you.

When you're an Alpha and he's an Alpha, you have two leaders and a lot of competition going on between the two of you.

Ever see a man when he's competing? He wants to win and he will do what it takes to make that happen. By coming from your softer, feminine side, which is your heart versus your mind, you can bring out the best in him.

Some women feel that over-giving to a man to make him happy will do this. Let me set the record straight by saying it doesn't!

Over giving is actually a masculine Alpha Quality. Our DNA comes from the caveman days where we as women needed protection and we needed a man to provide for us to survive.

These roles are still in your DNA coding and in his. When you over-give to a man, you are saying, *I'm the Alpha in the relationship.* It doesn't mean you can't give, of course you can. But when you over-give, after a while, you are perceived as a man's mother, not as his partner.

Yes...you are strong and we, as women, emotionally need to be strong for the family and the relationship. But when you do all the physical work and all the emotional work in the relationship, you don't leave room for a man to honor his DNA coding of doing for you. A man needs to be needed.

Let me reassure you that coming into your feminine power doesn't mean lying down like a doormat and just allowing a man to walk on you. Far from it! It means learning how to bring out the best in a man and in turn, he will bring out the best in you.

When I was finally able to let go of rubbing my strength and power in a man's face, I found men were stepping over themselves to help me. It didn't take anything away from me. It actually helped me get over the idea of, "I have to do it all," and it brought me into true partnership with men.

And you know what? That felt good. I ended up feeling cherished, adored and respected for being myself. And men would tell me that I was the best date they ever had. Why? Because I let him be the man he was meant to be.

Are You Bending Like A Pretzel To Please Him?

"A gentleman will open doors, pull out chairs, and carry things. Not because she's helpless or unable, but because he wants to show her that she is valuable and worthy of respect."
~Author Unknown

Bev had been with John for two years. When they first met, he'd do everything for her. It was great. In John's eyes, Bev could do no wrong and anything she wanted, he did his best to give her.

After a couple of months, she noticed him doing less and less for her. It felt like once the chase was over, so was he. He went back to his life and even though they went out and had fun, he stopped being so attentive.

She loved him and would do anything for him. In fact, Bev totally rearranged her life so she could be there whenever he was ready to play. She gave up her friends and the activities she loved doing because she thought this was the right thing to do.

She really wanted that attentive man back who was always happy and excited to see her. She wondered where he'd gone.

For some reason, as women, we think its ok to bend like a pretzel giving up what we love in our lives to accommodate a man's desires. We all do it because we care about a man and it feels natural to want to please him and make him happy.

Yet when you do this, you slowly start losing the interesting pieces of who you are. You become a female clone of the man you love, hanging out with his friends and participating in his activities and his life. As a result, your Inner Glow begins to dim.

You see, what makes you so attractive to a man in the first place is your uniqueness, your own passion and your own zeal for the life you created before him.

It's time to consider putting back in your life some of the activities and friends that made you so happy. Give your friends a call. They are usually pretty forgiving and happy to welcome you back into the fold.

As you change and find the *"real you"* again… The man you love will take notice and there's a good chance your renewed passion will once more excite him, ultimately, bringing back the spark that's been missing in you and your relationship.

Before we end this chapter, I want to make it clear that coming from your softer side is not about being weak. It's about coming into your true power. Instead of pushing or forcing a man to get your needs met, you are drawing him towards you by putting him in a position of stepping up to be the man he wants to be for you.

"Sometimes the girl who's always been there for everyone else, needs someone to be there for her."
~Author Unknown

LISA COPELAND

Step 3... Understanding Men

Who They Are And What They Want From The Woman They Date

Is He Your Type?

"You don't love someone for their looks, their clothes or their fancy car. You love them because they can sing a song only your heart can understand." ~Author Unknown

I want you to think about how many hours you've spent looking at men online thinking, this man is handsome but he's just not my type... He's not my religion... We live in different areas of our city... He's too old... He's too young... and the list goes on.

I remember thinking guys who were extremely athletic were not my type. I thought of them as narcissistic and judged them for wanting their bodies to be super toned.

My first online dating experience was with eHarmony. The dating site would continually match me with men who felt physical fitness was a top priority. I actually called and said, "Could you stop sending me these types of men?" They laughed, saying I was the only person EVER to do that.

I was so worried about being judged for my own body that I ended up judging them first. This way I couldn't be rejected just in case I wasn't toned to their standards.

The funny thing is I had no clue what their standards

were. I based my assumptions on fears that weren't even true. And the irony is that once I gave these guys a try, some of these so-called tone men showed up on a date with a huge belly.

The mistake I made was rejecting good men based on an assumption of what I thought they were looking for!

My client, Michelle ended up in a relationship with a wonderful man who was way out of her usual comfort zone when it came to religion and age. In the past, she'd always chosen to date men who appeared to be her usual type but she found herself in one unsuccessful relationship after another. Why?

Because what she truly desired was a man who could shower her with lots of affection and attention. The type of man she was always choosing wasn't able to do that.

They'd been men who were intellectual, which totally stimulated her mind but not her body and soul. The new man in her life was very loving and smart. He would do anything for her and for the first time ever, she felt really happy in a relationship. She didn't find herself yearning for that illusive something that had always been missing in the past.

It took going out of her comfort zone to finally find happiness with a man.

To find happiness and contentment in a relationship with a man, you may want to go outside your own comfort zone and try a different type of man than you're used to dating. When you think of the men you've dated or married in the past, do you find a common theme, something in their personality or background that was similar in each one?

We create dating patterns because certain types of men feel safe to us. It doesn't mean they are. In fact, they most of they time they aren't. But because they feel so comfortable, we continue going out with the same type over and over again unsuccessfully.

The next time you're browsing your favorite dating site, take a look at five men you may have passed up because they didn't fit your "what I want in a man" test.

Give yourself the opportunity to revisit them and see if there is anything that might now appear interesting to you. You may find yourself resisting these men – feeling a strong urge to go back to the kind of man you're used to.

"You can't start the next chapter of your life if you keep rereading your last one." ~Author Unknown

Start by giving yourself permission to feel uncomfortable and allow yourself to respond to one of these new men you'd have knocked out in the past.

When you open the door to someone who is different you'll give yourself the opportunity to experience happiness, compatibility and love with a new type of man.

Get back online and look at all types of men on there to date. The worst that can happen is you have a coffee date that goes nowhere. But the best may happen – you find exactly what you've been looking for but couldn't find in the type of man you usually dated.

Overcoming The Dilemma Of Attracting Your Ex Again

"Single doesn't have to mean lonely. Single simply means I'm resting my heart until its ready to love again." ~Author Unknown

Let's take a look at two different women with the same problem, attracting the same type of man repeatedly.

Anne...

Anne always seemed to attract the same type of man, an alcoholic who got drunk all the time and became mean and abusive to her. She was so tired of attracting this pattern over and over again. She came to me asking why this was happening and what she could do to change this.

One of the reason you'll continuously attract the same type of man is something inside you needs healing and only this **type** of man can help you do it. Often it originates from unresolved issues in your family of origin.

When I married hubby number one, my sister would say, "You know you married mom." I was shocked. As much as I tried to deny it… I came to realize she was right.

Not only did I do it once, I did it again when I married my second husband. It wasn't until I finally woke up and recognized that I needed to heal the wounds between my mom and myself that my relationships with men changed.

For Anne, one of the characteristics of an alcoholic is self-abuse. By attracting men like this, Anne needed to ask herself if she was doing anything abusive to herself that was being reflected by the men she chose to date and be in relationships with.

Doing this exercise was a gift for Anne. It was like a wake up call. She could either figure out what inside her needed healing and nurturing or she could continue being miserable dating the same men over and over again.

She chose to heal her heart and once she did, she ended up attracting a kinder man who reflected the nurturing she was giving herself.

Healing is not an overnight process. It takes time and some hard inner reflective work to change. But, doing the work can make a huge difference in your life in terms of attracting the men you really want and desire.

"People change for two reason: either they learn enough that they want to or they've been hurt enough that they have to."
–Author Unknown

Phyllis…

Phyllis is a 66-year-old woman who keeps attracting and inviting the wrong men into her life. She's attractive, healthy, outgoing, and still very active. She looks a lot younger than her age.

She found herself distraught over being alone so many years after her divorce. Her first marriage lasted 24 years and over the 19 years since then, she'd been engaged three times. But each one turned out to have major anger issues, some bordering on rage!

And each time, she didn't see this until she was madly in love with a man. That's when his rage would surface in their private life. She'd make mental excuses for each one, always asking them to get help.

She'd even offered to emotionally support them through counseling, but they'd all refused. After a while, she finally woke up and asked herself if this is what she wanted for the rest of her life.

Phyllis was a wonderful woman with her own interests and life. Her dream was to find a man who would enhance her life. Yet she kept choosing men with major rage issues she didn't see until she'd become emotionally bonded with them.

Rage is a personality disorder that cannot be changed with counseling unless a man wants to do something about changing it. RUN, don't walk, from this type of man.

If Phyllis had been honest with herself, she'd probably have noticed a man's anger flaring quickly in emails, phone calls or in the way each of these men interacted with others. She chose to ignore the red flags. Why?

She'd painted a picture in her head of who she thought a man was based on his profile. She fell in love with this picture and when the real man showed up it always surprised her.

Think about the men you're going to meet. Do you draw your own picture of who he is from a profile and a couple of dates? If you are doing this, it's easy to miss the "red flags."

You're wearing what I like to call the **"rose colored glasses,"** where you literally can't see a man's flaws until the glasses come off about six to 18 months into a relationship.

Be willing to look at who a man really is, not who you think he is.

You can do this by slowing down the dating process. Start observing what a man says and how he acts with you and with others. Write these observations down in a journal after every date.

Putting it on paper helps you see the real picture far more clearly. Your mind has a tendency to shift the facts to what you want them to be. Your observations will be the clues to who a man really is and whether he's a man you really want in your life.

What To Do When You Miss Your Ex

"I don't miss him. I miss who I thought he was."
-Author Unknown

How To Overcome No One Being As Good As "He" Was

Missy hadn't dated in years. When asked about it she'd say, "In all honesty, I can't find anyone worth dating." She'd had a pretty decent first marriage. Sadly, her husband, Ron, had died and she felt like she couldn't find anyone to replace what she'd had with him.

Missy did go online but looking at one picture after another of all the men on there, she still felt no one was as handsome as her husband had been. Her friends even tried fixing her up but the men she met seemed like old geezers even though they were her age.

Even though he'd been gone for ten years, Missy deeply missed her ex.

I shared with Missy that ten years is literally a lifetime ago. Ron was probably in his 40's at the time. That's still a pretty youthful age especially in appearance, which may explain why everyone now looked like an "old geezer" to her.

There is no way Missy can replace Ron. He was unique and her relationship with him was one of a kind with its own set of qualities special to the two of them.

Missy could find someone to share life with if she'd let Ron stop being the standard a man had to live up to. Over the past ten years, her needs in a relationship have changed. If she can get in touch with what they presently are versus going by what they were in the past, she could find a new man to share her life with. If she continues on the path she's on, it's likely she's destined to being alone the rest of her life.

Going Back to Your Ex Usually Doesn't Work Either

"When people walk away from you, let them go. Your destiny is never tied to anyone who leaves you and it doesn't mean they are bad people. It just means that their part in your story is over."
–Author Unknown

Alice broke up with her boyfriend Alex after being together for two years. She just couldn't see herself being in a relationship with him a decade from now.

After two months, she began to miss him. And every time Alex wrote to Alice, he'd express the most beautiful thoughts, causing her heart to long for him even more. She felt maybe she'd made a mistake breaking up with him and wondered whether she should go back and try again.

Alice was experiencing one of the loneliest times in her life, the ending of a relationship. Life changes from being part of a couple to being single again and it's a huge adjustment.

When you experience this profound type of loneliness, it makes the person you left behind seem better than they really are.

There's also a certain feeling of safety with an ex. You know him for the good, the bad and the ugly. After a breakup, as time passes and you find yourself alone, you forget what was so irritating about him. There is a tendency to only remember the good stuff, which means you end up turning the *ex* into the *saint* he's not.

To overcome the sainting of an ex, take a few moments and write a list of all the ways your ex annoyed you and all the ways he made you happy.

Replacing an ex right away will divert you from always thinking about him. But you're still left with open wounds from this relationship that need healing. You really do want to take as much time as you need before dating again.

When you don't, you bring your unresolved emotions about another man into the new relationship. Plus when you haven't done the work needed to heal, you usually end up attracting the same type of man with the same type of issues right back into your life. He's just wearing different clothing and has a different job.

Over time, when emotions cool down, you might consider becoming friends with your ex. While you're healing, it's healthier if you don't have contact with him because it constantly reconnects you the two of you, which I'll talk about later in the chapter, Breaking Up: Are You Addicted To An Ex?

There's nothing wrong with asking an ex to stop communicating with you for a while. You can share with him that you're in the process of healing and just need some time alone to sort out your feelings.

I know this can be a difficult time. And if you're like most couples who try to get back together, you'll find your chemistry to be off the charts. Lust can be mistaken for love here. But unless you think whatever broke you up has changed, it's likely you'll find the same issues still there once the hormonal urges settle down.

Is An Old Flame Worth Checking Out If He's Single?

"There's a guy out there who's going to be really happy that you didn't get back together with your crappy ex-boyfriend."

~Author Unknown

Lori was going on divorce number two. Her first marriage happened when she was 21 and lasted 20 years. After being single for a couple of years, she met Robert and together they had a nine-year relationship, three of them as husband and wife. Then one day, Robert walked out of the relationship without warning.

The nights were lonely for Lori, so to fill her time she cruised Facebook and ended up finding Jonathan, her old high school boyfriend. Over the years, Jonathan had made several attempts to apologize to Lori for his less than perfect behavior when they were together as kids.

They did reconnect and she found out he'd become quite

successful in business. She liked this idea. Feeling financial security was something any woman her age would want in a man she dated.

Jonathan told her he'd been married three times but not one had lasted more than five years. In his mind, no one had ever been able to take Lori's place. He'd realized what a fool he'd been in high school and begged her for a second chance at this time in their lives.

In high school, Lori had been quite attracted to him but as he stood in front of her looking more like his father than the man she had dated in her teens, she was finding it hard to reconnect with him.

Old flames can rekindle memories from a special time in your life when you were young and fell in love for the first time. Yet if you haven't seen this man in quite a while, you can be taken aback by his appearance. It often doesn't jive with the man you remember falling in love with.

If you give the reacquainting process some time, you'll be able to find that young man you knew way back when. It will feel sweet and you'll come to recognize the young man you fell in love with in your teens most likely still lives inside this older man.

However, you are both different people from who you were 30 plus years ago. And you both come to the table with kids, grandkids and a slew of baggage you weren't even aware existed back then.

Can it work? Yes, I've seen couples get together 30 years later. But most do what Lori did. Check the old sweetie out and head down memory lane only to find the attraction nonexistent after 50.

But… you never know. The best that can happen is the two of you click and you explore a relationship. The worst? It doesn't work but you've gotten the gift of reliving a very sweet time in your life and this can be a really nice feeling.

How To Tell If You're Dating A Married Man

"You love me right?

Sure, I do, just don't call or text me after 5 PM or weekends. That's when I'm with my wife and kids."

~Rottenecards

You meet the greatest guy online. He contacts you without a picture but in his email, he offers to send you one. You like what you see when he does and you decide to connect.

Turns out you have a lot in common and somehow the two of you never seem to run out of subjects to talk about. The conversations flow so easily. He's amazing and you feel like you've never met anyone quite like him.

He tells you that he travels for his job during the week so he often calls you from his hotel room. The two of you talk until the wee hours of the night sharing the stories of your lives that day. You begin looking forward to these nightly calls and miss them when they don't happen.

He rarely calls you on the weekend and sometimes the two of you will be talking when his phone suddenly disconnects. You call him back and it goes right to voice mail. He tells you his battery ran out of juice.

"You can tell by a woman's title whether she is married (Miss and Mrs.), but not by a man's (Mr.); as if getting married is so life-changing for a woman that her identity is changed for all of society to know and approve." ~Author Unknown

You feel yourself falling for this special man and you really want to meet him but he skirts the issue whenever you bring it up, changing the subject to how *awesome* you are and how much he cares about you.

When a scenario like this happens where a man talks but won't meet, you are probably dating a married man.

The telltale signs for determining whether a man's married are...

• **He doesn't post a picture online but is willing to send you one in an email. He doesn't want his wife's single friends telling her he's online cheating on her.**
• **He calls from hotels because it's safe. He won't get caught. The question to ask yourself is... Does he call you when he's not traveling? If not, why not? Probably because he's married.**

- He rarely calls on weekends. Why? Because he's with his significant other who probably keeps him busy.
- Your calls drop off suddenly out of nowhere. Chances are his wife is walking in the room.
- He evades your questions about when the two of you can meet, changing the subject to the special qualities he's noticed about you. It's a diversion tactic and he's playing into the fact women love hearing good things about themselves.

If you speak with or meet a man and these signs show up, don't hesitate to ask a man if he's married or divorced. If he can't give you a definite "I am single," then consider letting him go. The chances of him leaving his wife for you are slim to none.

You'll be the one sitting at home always waiting for him to call. And ultimately, this will break your heart. It's worth your while to let a man like this go. It's a dead end for you.

Get yourself back online and start dating men who want to meet you after a couple of calls. Meeting is the only way you'll be able to tell if you're truly a fit for each other.

A phone call relationship is a fantasy one and can feel like the perfect relationship. It's not!

So You Love An Older Man...

"Men do not quit playing because they grow old;
they grow old because they quit playing."

~Oliver Wendell Holmes

Pamela, a single, 56-year-old woman, dated off and on for three years before she met Alan, the 67-year-old man she's currently with. Before Alan, she'd dated Steve.

Pamela's dates with Steve were fun and had included a lot of kissing and some minor touchy feely play. But Steve and Pamela both realized they were not meant to be in a romantic relationship with each other so they formed a great friendship and began meeting for lunch once or twice a month.

About a year later, Pamela began dating Alan. Alan was not happy with Pamela's friendship with another man and felt Steve was being disrespectful to him by seeing his girlfriend on a regular basis.

Pamela was having a hard time with this and couldn't understand why seeing her friend Steve was such a big deal for Alan. She was not romantically interested in Steve at all but couldn't seem to make Alan understand this.

Many over 50's men and women stay friends with people they've briefly dated. Often a romantic relationship won't work but a plutonic one does quite well.

Alan is a member of the Silent Generation, the generation born prior to Baby Boomers. He comes from a generation where honor, respect and doing the right thing are part of their core.

Alan would likely be willing to lay down his life for Pamela. That's how deep honor and respect run in these men. In Alan's eyes, Steve is being disrespectful of Alan's territory, which Pamela is considered to be part of.

Boomers view life differently than many from the generation before them. They grew up with "free love" and "give peace a chance" and this can create conflict over how core value issues are dealt with.

Dating an older man has its pluses. He will be chivalrous, opening the door for you, helping you with your coat, wanting to pay for what he can afford. He is a man's man. The downside is… he is far more territorial than a boomer man.

He will want you to himself. In this situation, if Pamela wants to take her relationship with Alan to the next level, she will probably have to give up her friendship to Steve.

Men born before 1945 grew up differently than you did if you're a Boomer woman. His energy might be different than yours and his health could become worrisome for you down the road. But so could the health of a Boomer man.

These older men are in a different phase of their life. They are slowing down as they move into retirement while you may be coming into yourself and your true-life purpose, thanks to menopause.

Older men are wonderful in their own right. They will make you feel like such a lady but they will be different in how they view life. They are worth trying out at least once on your dating adventure.

Ready To Have Fun Being A Cougar?

"Love Knows No Age!" *~Author Unknown*

To be or not to be a "cougar!" This is the question for women over 50!

Who would have thought in this day and age that you'd have so many options to choose from when it comes to dating and men? Believe it or not – lots of men want to date you – older men, men closer to your age and now younger men are trying to catch your eye.

I must admit the last one, known as "cougar dating," thanks to the now defunct marriage of Demi Moore and Ashton Kutcher, was a little hard for me to wrap my head around. Yes, I'd dated men three to five years younger but 10 to 20 would take some getting used to.

Online, younger men wrote me all the time and I'd always say, "Are you looking for a mom?" They'd quickly tell me, "No way!" They just felt younger women were too high maintenance for them and had far too much drama going on in their lives.

I had to laugh at the consistent high maintenance comments that I heard time and time again from these young men. They just have no idea what it takes to look good at 50.

Hair alone can be a full time job whether it's plucking it from places you never knew hair could grow or coloring it constantly just to hide the grey.

As a woman over 50, you probably aren't heading over to the local *Steak And Shake* to meet a date. It's more likely you want to be wined and dined at nicer restaurants, something these young men can't necessarily afford unless they have a trust fund.

Let's face it – between our hair and our taste for the finer things in life – high maintenance is still very much a part of our lives. It's just been hidden from these young men since they haven't lived with their moms in a long time.

Fortunately for you, these young ones have created a fantasy in their brains of who they think we are as older women. And who are we to change this image? They can be a lot of fun and if a lot of sex is what you want, they are the men who will provide it for you. Just be safe!

It feels GREAT when a younger man asks you out and thinks you're hot! It's a huge ego boost especially from men who are in their 40's.

These men are surrounded daily by young women with their smooth complexions and their youthful glow. Yet here he is willing to skip all that because he thinks you're pretty cool, you're calm and low maintenance, even with wrinkles around your eyes. Imagine that?

Anna, a 55 year old woman literally bumped into this gorgeous late 30's, early 40's young man who was a cross between Hugh Laurie and George Clooney. They started talking and he invited her to have a drink. They sat for hours laughing and sharing all kinds of stories.

Next thing she knew, he was asking her out. She was momentarily stunned – this handsome young stud wanted a date with her? He could have had the pick of the litter his own age and even younger, yet he was asking her, a 50 plus year old woman on a date.

She wanted to burst out laughing but instead played his game and flirted with him. She had a charming afternoon being courted by a young handsome man. In the end, Anna did not go out with him.

As much chemistry as they had, she actually found it hard to relate to a lot of what he was saying but that afternoon was fun and time well spent in her mind. Plus, he sure did make her feel good!

The Bad Boy

"A woman has got to love a bad man once or twice in her life, to be thankful for a good one."

~Marjorie Kinnan Rawlings

Let's talk about the man every woman over 50 is still wildly attracted to… THE BAD BOY! He's the very handsome man who makes you feel alive inside and unbelievably wonderful about yourself.

He paints the best pictures of the life the two of you can have together.

He knows women well and he knows what to say and

what to do to make you his. He will tell you that you are beautiful or that they broke the mold when they made you.

He will tell you there is no one else he can trust or share his deepest thoughts with other than you.

A *Bad Boy* knows just what to say to make you his and you feel honored he chose you above everyone else to be his girlfriend. You fall in love with him based on his words, his handsome face and the chemistry between you that feels off the charts.

He'll say I love you one day then the next, he'll be gone because the *Bad Boy* can't make a commitment to anyone. He loves going after the woman he wants but once captured, he quickly tires and starts looking for someone he thinks might be better. And he'll come back to do it again between his relationships.

He'll woo you once more telling you what you mean to him and how much he misses you. You hope this will be the time he'll stay with you. He doesn't want to be alone so he'll use you until he finds his next prey.

He'll break your heart again and again until you finally decided to stop this heart-breaking cycle.

A tell-tale sign of the *Bad Boy* is his extremes in life. He's often very handsome and very masculine. He has to have the best in liquor, cars and women. He's often extremely wealthy and extremely fast in whatever he does. He's quite exciting and often very self- indulgent.

He'll make you miserable in the long run because he'll

shut you out without a second thought. I know. I lived this with an old flame of mine from high school who came back into my life after my divorce.

He told me how he would put me on a pedestal if we were together. He'd paint these romantic scenarios telling me how he had never stopped loving me. This would go on for weeks at a time. Then he'd vanish, only to reappear then vanish again. Each time, I'd hope this was it but of course it wasn't.

Finally, I came to realize, like most *Bad Boys*, his words were hollow. There was no action behind them and there never would be. This is when I decided to change course and look for a man who would capture my heart and want to keep it.

There are a lot of good men out there who may be less handsome or less quick on their feet who would love a chance to date you. Unlike the *Bad Boy,* this man follows up his words with action and that's what will make you feel safe and cared for in a relationship. In the long run, this is something a bad boy with all of his charm is incapable of doing.

Why Men Over 50 Are So Quick To Put A Ring On Your Finger

"Time decides... who you meet in life, the heart decides... who you want in your life, but behavior decides... who remains in your life!" ~Author Unknown

Another amazing thing has happened as you've aged. Women over 50 can now date however many men they want as often as they want... even all of them at the same time if they desire. But men over 50 seem to want to settle down right away and have a great relationship sharing their life with one woman. A huge role reversal, isn't it?

As we talked about in the last chapter, the players are still out there but most of the men over 50 I've spoken with truly desire a good committed relationship with ONE woman whom they can please and make happy.

A man seems to know fairly quickly whether he thinks you're a good woman for him. When this happens, he can become quite aggressive about snapping you up and taking you off the market so you won't be available to anyone else.

Even though it freaks you out, it's actually a compliment to you!

The problem arises when you and he aren't on the same dating page. He feels rejected for putting himself in the vulnerable position of letting you know how he feels.

He doesn't understand why you would be on a dating site if you weren't looking for love with one person like he is. So he gets mad when you want to date a couple of men to figure out who Mr. Right is.

If a man does this to you, all you have to do is slow down the process.

Let him know how much you've enjoyed your time together so far. Talk about how much fun it will be getting to know each other to see where this relationship might go, and that you're excited to figure this out with him over time.

If you don't like him or he seems *needy*, let him know you appreciate the compliment but at this point, you aren't ready for a serious relationship with anyone.

This will let him down easy. Chances are he's looking for an emotional connection that leads to marriage. So he will probably leave you alone and start hunting for another woman who will better fit his needs.

Most dating sites ask what type of relationship you're looking for, whether it's a date, a committed relationship, or marriage. This will create a filter that helps you attract the type of man who wants the same kind of connection as you do.

Patrick saw Andrea's picture online and knew deep in his heart she could be the one. He loved her smile and found her profile to be fun and refreshing compared to what he'd seen posted by other women on the site.

He emailed her immediately hoping she'd write back to him. She did and they moved their new friendship to the phone. He loved her voice and couldn't wait to meet her so he suggested they meet at an expensive restaurant in their area. He really wanted to impress her.

They met on New Year's Day. Patrick took this as a sign

this could be a new beginning for him. When Andrea showed up, Patrick thought she looked *fantastic* and even better than the picture he'd seen of her online.

He was tired of dating and wanted her to be his girlfriend starting tonight! He asked if he could order for them and she said yes, so he went all out ordering food he thought she'd like.

A couple behind them noticed all this and the four of them started talking. Patrick felt like he and Andrea had been together forever. It felt that good. When the end of the night came, Patrick sat back in his chair and smiled, feeling such satisfaction with this beautiful woman sitting in front of him.

He took her hand and said, "Andrea, I think you're great. How would you feel about seeing each other exclusively?"

Andrea was taken aback. She didn't anticipate this. She barely knew him and would have been happy to hear, "Would you like to go out with me on a second date?"

She thanked him for a lovely evening, telling him that she wasn't ready to commit to being a girlfriend after only one date. Patrick was floored, then he got mad and suggested they go. He walked Andrea to her car and never called her again.

I can't begin to tell you the number of times I've heard this story. Men moving really fast and women feeling scared by their neediness and intensity. A man has a picture in his head of the woman he believes he wants.

If you fit this picture, he's not going to waste time letting you get away and he will do all he can to catch you as his girlfriend.

A big tipoff that he's thinking you're girlfriend material is the **expensive restaurant** he's chosen to impress you with on a first date.

One last thing about an expensive first date… there are men trying to impress you who might expect sex in return for taking you somewhere nice. Be prepared for this by having boundaries in place for when you're willing to begin a sexual relationship with a man. We'll talk more about this in a later chapter.

Are You Turning Men Off Without Realizing It?

"Life offers wisdom generously. Everything teaches. Not everyone learns." ~ Rachel Naomi Rernen

Have you been out on a date with a man where it feels like everything is going smoothly? The conversation is easy. You're having fun. Then out of nowhere, he just ends the date abruptly and you have no idea why.

You replay the date in your mind over and over again wondering what went wrong? I've spoken with a lot of men and consistently they've shared five specific behaviors women do that turn them off in the dating process.

Turn Off #1… Hiding Your Feminine Side

If you're in a high-power job and you schedule a first date right after work, it may be hard to make a smooth emotional transition from work to dating.

Without realizing it, you can easily fall back into work mode giving orders to a man about what you'd like him to do for you. To a man this comes across as masculine behavior, and let me assure you, if he's straight, he's not looking for another man to be his partner in life.

If you find you have a difficult time transitioning from work to play, be sure you spend some time decompressing before a date, otherwise you might find your Mr. Right looking for a more feminine Ms. Right.

Turn Off #2... Bashing Your Ex on a First Date

Early in the dating game, a new man doesn't want to hear how bitter and angry you may still feel about your ex. To a man this feels like three are on the date, not just the two of you, and he feels he has to compete for better or worse with your ex to win you over.

It's too much work for him so it's likely he'll choose to move on. If you are having trouble getting over the pain from your last relationship, it's a good idea to seek help from a professional before you begin dating again.

Turn Off #3... Inquiring Mind's Want to Know!

The quickest way to scare a man off at the beginning of the dating process is by asking him "none of your business type questions" about his life. These are **privacy invading** questions like, "What time did you get up today?" "What did you do last night?" or "Where are you going?"

Men love the freedom to do as they please. When a man feels like you're keeping tabs on his activities, he starts thinking you're trying to take his freedom away and that you will try and control his life.

> *"I won't block you or delete you. I'm keeping you there, so you're able to see how happy I am without you." ~Author Unknown*

This feels really scary to a man!

When he's ready, he'll fill you in on his activities. In the meanwhile, take this time to enjoy your own life instead of wanting to know so much about his.

Turn Off #4... Being Attached At The Hip

Nothing scares a man faster than a woman who wants to spend every waking hour of her day with him, especially if it happens right after you've met. To a man this appears as if you don't have a life and that you're looking to turn his life into yours.

After only one date, if you find yourself making plans for the two of you that stretch out over the next year, this is going to be a problem. Wanting too much of his time right away just makes you appear like a clingy and emotionally needy woman, which is scary to a man.

In reality, men are most attracted to women who are

confident, independent and have lives of their own they bring to the dating table.

Turn Off #5... Saying The "L" Word Too Soon

Sometimes we find ourselves having intense feelings for a new man in our life and we use the words "I love you" far too quickly.

It's a good idea to keep this feeling to yourself until you've been dating a while or until he says the "L" word first. If you say it before he's ready, you could find yourself right back in the dating pool again.

> *"Falling in love is easy. But staying in love is very special."*
> *~Author Unknown*

Two Important Reasons Why He Might Not Call You Back

You Aren't His Type

Do you carry a specific picture in your mind of the man you'd like to spend the rest of your life with? Most of us do so it shouldn't be surprising when I tell you men do as well. In fact, when a man contacts you, it's because he believes you and the picture in his head just might be a match.

The two of you spend hours on the phone. He starts

talking out loud sharing thoughts with you like, "We'll have to get you out here on one of my horses," or "We'll have to try out the latest Japanese restaurant in your area since you love sushi so much."

His picture is working overtime, thinking you might be the one and you get excited thinking maybe he's right for you too! Then the two of you meet. And within minutes he's decided you aren't a match to the picture of the woman he wants, so the second date doesn't happen.

When this happens don't take it personally. It's just the pictures in his head of whom he thinks he wants and who you are do not match. This is why you want to limit emails and phone calls prior to meeting a new man. You don't want to get yourself emotionally invested in an imaginary relationship with a man you have yet to meet.

"Stop chasing love, affection, or attention. If another person doesn't give it freely, it isn't worth having."
~Author Unknown

You Have Sex With A Man Too Quickly!

You meet a man, the chemistry is hot and as the date ends, the two of you start kissing and kissing and kissing some more.

Hands start roving all over the place and you find yourself in the back seat of the car having sex with a man you've only known a couple of hours.

You're both on fire. In this moment, it feels good and it feels right. When it's over, he kisses you and says, "I'll call you" but he doesn't. Why? The sex was too easy for him to get.

You want to understand that men categorize the women they date into two groups. The first are the women they play with, as in first date sex or friends with benefits situations. It's easy sex, it's fun for him but that's all it is.

Beware! Having sex on a first date rarely leads to a long term relationship with a man.

Then there is the second category, the woman he considers as **potential relationship material.** This is where he thinks the two of you might be a match.

So if you want to make it to category number two, promise yourself, even when your hormones are raging, that you'll slow it down. Hold off having sex and this means anything beyond kissing until you think a real relationship is a possibility.

There are all kinds of reasons men don't call back… Some are as silly as a mannerism you display that reminds him of his ex. Save yourself a lot of date analysis and evaluation by not taking a first date personally and by not being invested in how it's going to turn out.

If it's meant to be, it will be and if it's not, chalk it up to an opportunity to spend some time with a new and interesting person that day.

Who Is That Drama Queen Men Always Write About?

"A real woman avoids drama, she knows her time is precious and she's not wasting it on unimportant things."

~Author Unknown

If you've been online, you've seen enough profiles to know that a lot of men write in their profiles about having no interest in the *drama queens* out there. Have you ever wondered just who this *drama queen* is?

Ladies, I want to fill you in by sharing this secret with you. Apparently, a *drama queen* is male code for *don't bring your past with ex's, friends and family to the dating table.*

You see there are a few women out there who have ruined it for the rest of us by using dates to rehash their issues with men from their past.

Remember, a man feels he has to fix your problems. It's literally in his DNA to rescue you as a "damsel in distress." Yet deep inside, a man knows when it comes to ex's, he can't fix these issues for you.

Unable to fix this, he thinks he's going to look like a failure in your eyes when nothing's even happened between the two of you.

You, on the other hand, might be bringing him your so-called "drama," only looking to get a man's perspective on the situation. He just doesn't see it this way unless you specifically ask him for his help in solving one problem, not ten problems that you're having.

If you're in a relationship with a good man and issues with men in your world come up, he will be there to support you and help you find solutions to fix what's wrong. But in the world of first, second and third dates, it's better to go elsewhere for advice about men who are troublesome for you.

What Every Woman Needs To Know About The Men They Want To Date After 50

"Dating is really hard because everyone puts on a front. It's really difficult to see who is who, so it is important to be yourself."
~Brooke Burke

Don't laugh, but one of my very favorite TV shows is *Survivor*. There were two seasons where the game pitted family members against each other. The pairs that touched me the most were the couples forced to be on opposite teams.

It's heart-wrenching to see how much it tears a man apart to watch his wife be in danger when there is nothing he can do about it. I want you to understand how important it is to a man that he makes you feel safe and protected.

Growing up, we weren't taught who men really are and what makes them tick. I know I wasn't and, in the past, I made huge mistakes led me to where I am now helping women really understand who men are... especially men over 50.

It starts with appreciating exactly who a man is. Men are wonderful but they aren't women. They don't think like women nor do they communicate like women. You can't expect a man to act like a woman or you're guaranteed to be disappointed.

Men over 50 are very masculine and they love when you bring this trait out in them. They'll show you how much they care about you through their actions.

Hollywood has messed with our heads on this one leading us to believe that men's idea of romance is Tom Cruise's character in the movie, *Jerry McGuire*. Think back to professing his love using the romantic words, "You complete me."

Real men are not about words. They show you their love by cutting your grass and giving you their coats when you're cold. If you expect love to come in words ... you could be waiting a very long time.

Men want to give to you. Let them open the door for you or change that light bulb you can't reach. It makes them feel good about themselves when they please you.

This leads us to criticizing a man for the job he is doing for you. He's doing his best and, yes, you may be able to do it better or faster than he can but don't. It makes him feel emasculated. If he has offered to do something for you, allow him to do it his way. Otherwise, the next time you ask for help, he'll tell you to hire a handyman. He doesn't want the aggravation of not being able to do anything right for you.

I can't begin to tell you how many men shared with me how much they dislike women who make demands in profiles or in person about things like salary requirements or restaurants you want to be taken to in order to date you. Men have had enough demands put on them at work and from their ex's. The last thing they want to do is meet yours before you've even met.

Men also expressed how tired they are of being remodeled by women. They are not interested in being your pet project.

You'll want to find a man you can accept for who he is. Otherwise, let him go and move on to someone who is more like the man you want.

Did you know how insecure men really are, especially when it comes to asking you out on a date? Having been rejected time and time again by so many women, they aren't moving too quick when it comes to putting themselves back in a vulnerable position…unless it feels safe to do so.

If you like a man, encourage him with eye contact and a warm smile or favor him online to let him know you're interested.

Remember, men weren't given a Dating Rulebook with their divorce papers either. So be kind to them and understand that as scared as you feel about dating, most of them are too.

Step 4... Getting A Clear Vision Of The Man You Want In Your Life

Who He Is And Why You Want Him

Who's Really Out There For You To Date?

"Beware of Destination Addiction-a preoccupation with the idea that happiness is the next place, the next job and the next partner. Until you give up the idea that happiness is somewhere else, it will never be where you are."
~Author Unknown

Now it's time to get a CLEAR VISION of the men you'd like to date. Let's start with age, which we touched on in the previous section. What age group of men interests you most?

We'll review for a moment…there are younger men contacting women over 50 online daily hoping to find a real relationship with them. Many young men appreciate an older woman for her experience and her wisdom.

Younger men can be fun. With their physical stamina they can keep up with you in all kinds of activities. They have more balanced masculine and feminine sides and seem to have a better understanding of feelings – something we as women love in a man.

I've personally seen successful relationships with this pairing. If older men can date younger women, why can't older women date younger men? It's worth trying out if you are game!

"Soul mates are people who bring out the best in you. They are not perfect but are always perfect for you." ~Author Unknown

If you want to feel really young and sexy, date an older man. These men come from a generation where they were taught to treat women like ladies.

Mothers whose only job in life was to please their husband and take care of the family raised them while fathers provided for the family and made sure the females were safe and protected. Something they taught their sons to do as well.

These men can bring out your most feminine essence. Men this age truly want to make you happy anyway they can and they will treasure you as the ONLY woman in their lives.

Men in their 60's and 70's fit this bill. And being close to the age of boomers where you both experienced the same world events happening in your lifetimes, you will have lots to talk about. Give these gentlemen a chance too. They're worth it!

Then you have the men who are our age. Believe it or not, most are *not* looking for a younger woman. What they really want is a woman between three to five years of their age.

These men want to have life experience in common with the woman they love, which they can't get with a 20, 30 or 40 year old. They may not open the door for you like an older man would, but you should have a lot in common with this man since you grew up in the same era.

Take advantage of this trend of having choice when it comes to the men you want to date. Enjoy the experience with each one and see which age group you like best in your life. You don't have to marry them. You can just have fun!

What Type Of Man Do You Want To Date and Be In Relationship With?

"The Perfect Guy is not the one who has the most money or is the most handsome one you'll meet. He's the one who knows how to make you smile and will take care of you each and every day until the end of time." ~Author Unknown

Are you looking for a man you feel is "your type" or who has a certain look? Have you ever considered looking at men as a total package, evaluating everything they have to offer to a relationship versus using only looks or job as the main criteria for dating them?

You'll want to ask yourself questions like these when determining whether or not this man has long-term relationship potential.

1. Will he bring you soup when you're sick?
2. Will he stop at the store and get you what you need even if it is a bit out of the way?
3. Will he bring you flowers and tell you he loves you even when it's not your birthday?
4. Will he rearrange his schedule to drive you to the airport so you don't have to hoist that suitcase out of your car or worry about parking before and after your trip?
5. When you've had a hard day, will he rub your back or bring you a glass of wine and give you a much-needed hug?
6. When you're dating, will he take your trash out to the curb so you don't have to?
7. Will he get up and do the dishes after dinner?
8. And, most importantly, will he look in your eyes like you are the best thing that ever happened to him?

As you're aging, you're probably going to want more in a partner than just his looks. You'll need more from a man in terms of support, especially in your golden years.

I watched my father take care of my mother as she was dying. He wiped her brow, took her to her chemo treatments, made her soup, and held her hand when she was scared.

My father is adorable – just ask my friends – but he would never have been the most handsome man on the block and would probably have been passed over online by lots of women.

Yet once women get to know him, it's his kindness and the

love he radiates from within that women of all ages adore about him.

"Some of the biggest challenges in relationships come from the fact that most people enter a relationship in order to get something: they're trying to find someone who's going to make them feel good. In reality, the only way a relationship will last is if you see your relationship as a place that you go to give, not a place that you go to take." ~Anthony Robbins

I can't deny looks are nice. They are. But next time you're reading those online profiles and you are thinking, *hmm, not so cute*, dig a little deeper and pay attention to what a man is saying in his profile.

If he writes that he's kind, caring, loves his animals, his kids and his grandkids – even when he's not the most handsome guy on the page, he's worth considering.

He's probably a man with a wonderful heart and a man whose looks could very well grow on you. After getting to know him, he may be like my father is – cute, loving and there for you through thick and thin.

You'll want to decide if it's a "looker" or a "Quality Man" you'd like to spend the rest of your life with.

How Rose Colored Glasses Affect Your Dating Vision

"Note to Self: There's an inner voice that knows the truth. Listen to her." ~Author Unknown

Cathy was married for 36 years to a wonderful man who passed away. Since then, she'd had a couple of not so great relationships. In her mind, she was not attracting the right guys.

When she looked back, she realized each one had given her clues to who they were but for some reason, she couldn't recognize them at the time.

Cathy was beginning to feel like she was leading from her heart, seeing only the good in each man. She was wondering if she should be using more of her head where the good and the not so good of these men might be more visible to her.

She was tired of getting hurt in her relationships and wasn't sure how to stop this cycle.

Instead of having a really clear vision of the men she'd like to date, she'd go dates wearing a pair of rose-colored glasses. Every man seemed like the catch of the century based on his profile, when in reality he wasn't.

This is why Cathy and so many women get hurt in the dating game. A man seems heavenly when you meet. You become exclusive quickly. You fall in love. Then boom... his real self suddenly shows up.

It feels like the little red flags that were always there just jumped out of nowhere and surprised you.

What's happening is beneath those rose colored glasses you're painting a picture in your mind of who a man is versus seeing the truth until it is too late. By the time you figure it out, you've gotten far too involved with a man.

The key is knowing what you want in a man before you start dating. You do this by making a **"Wish List"** of the qualities a man needs to have to date you. Keep this list close at hand, and compare it to what a man says about himself in both his profile and in person.

After your date, go home and write down what you heard him say. This will give you the black and white clues to who he is. Then compare him to your list to see if he matches most of the qualities you desire in a man.

This little exercise gives you the ability to choose whether a man is right for you based on what he tells you, not on the pretty picture you've created in your mind of who you think he is.

What Are Your Deal Breakers?

"The trick is finding someone who complements you instead of completes you. You need to be complete on your own."
~Author Unknown

To get a clear vision of the man you desire, begin by figuring out the qualities a man "must have" to date you, such as a love of pets or the same religion or culture as you.

Next, you'll want to figure out your Deal Breakers. They're qualities you can't tolerate and don't want in your life, such as smoking. You want to limit them to no more than 20. More than 20, you're looking for a perfection that just doesn't exist.

Potential Deal Breakers List

Smoking
Addictive behaviors
Minor children
Age
Adult child lives with a man
Pets
Religion
Politics
Jobs
Educational level
Number of marriages
Health general including STD's
Mental health
Race/culturally
Treat others/wait staff
Money
Retired
Working out/Level of activity

Men also have **Deal Breakers** when it comes to dating. But the difference between you and a man is men honor their Deal Breakers. You'll see this when a man is in a relationship with a woman for years and years but won't marry her. In his mind, she has a Deal Breaker that isn't suitable for marriage.

We as women have a tendency not to honor our Deal Breakers when it comes to men. We think with a little work and a lot of love… we can change him and all will be well in our world.

This just isn't true. Men don't change unless they want to change.

You might say, "But I love him so much." If this is the case and he has one of your Deal Breakers, you aren't honoring yourself. You would be settling. So many women choose to settle with a man loaded with Deal Breakers because they're afraid no one else is out there to date and be in relationship with.

This is an illusion. Your mind is playing tricks on you. All it does is take you to a place of scarcity when it comes to men. Yet these days, with our age group leading the pack with the highest number of divorces, there is actually an abundance of men out there for you to date.

All you have to do is go to a mainstream dating site and you'll see thousands of men right in your area looking for a woman just like you if you're willing to give him a chance.

Now, let's take a moment and talk about some of the most common Deal Breakers worth thinking about.

Pets or No Pets… If you have a beloved Fluffy or Fido in your life, then you'll want a man who'll treasure your "baby" like you do.

Children… Whether they are adults or minors, you'll want to figure out where your relationship fits into the family of origin equation. And if they are minor children are you willing to deal with those teenage years again especially if your kids are now adults?

Smokers… I once had a boyfriend who'd take himself outside in all kinds of weather for a smoke. He'd stand outside my garage door and puff away. Then he'd come in and wash his face before getting near me.

This was his way of showing me his love. It was nice but for me, it became a major Deal Breaker for future relationships. Regardless of what he did, he still smelled like smoke and I can't seem to tolerate this smell.

Religion… Do you need a man in your life who can share your religious beliefs, going to church or temple with you on a regular basis?

Alcohol Use… Are members of Alcohol Anonymous okay for you to date or do you want someone you can share a glass of wine with at the end of the day?

Differences in Sexual Behavior… Decide whether you want a full-blown *Fifty Shades of Grey* relationship, sex once a year on your birthday or somewhere in between.

Money Issues and Differences… Do you want him to pay for everything for both of you? Or can he be financially responsible just for his share?

Take some time to clear your head and really think about the specifics of your Deal Breakers and what each one actually means to you. I guarantee whatever Deal Breakers you skip over now will become major conflicts in your relationship at a later date.

It's better to know whether he has your Deal Breakers before you get to far into your relationship and you're emotionally connected to a man who may not be right for you.

While you're thinking about it, why don't you take a few moments and write your own Deal Breaker List right now?

As you get to know a man, refer back to this list to see if he has the qualities it takes to be with you. And remember, if a healthy long-term relationship is what you really desire in your life, then you'll want to choose a man who doesn't have one of the Deal Breakers on your list.

How To Tell If He's Mr. Right

"Where there is no vision, dreams perish." ~*Author Unknown*

You want to find the great man you just know is out there waiting for you. You date and date… Then suddenly, one shows up who has long-term relationship potential going for him.

He's passed the test when it comes to your Dating Wish List and Deal Breaker List. You've enjoyed spending time together and you'd like to see if the two of you can take it to the next level.

The first question you want to ask yourself is do you like who he is? It's so easy to get caught up in the **chemistry** when you first meet someone. And when an intimate relationship happens quickly, it's even harder to figure out if what you heart's feeling is lust or love. When a woman has a physical relationship with a man, her heart and her body bond with him making it easy to mistake what emotion she's feeling.

This is when you want to take a step back and ask yourself some important questions about this man.

Questions like...

- Do you like the way he treats you?
- Do you like the way he treats others in the world like friends, family or even the wait staff of your favorite restaurant?
- Does he show you that he wants to make you happy?
- Do you like how the two of you communicate together?
- Do you enjoy spending time together? When disagreements come up, how do the two of you handle them?

It's much easier to fall in "love" than it is to fall in "like." Yet liking the man in your life for exactly who he is will be the main ingredient for success in the long-term relationship you're looking for.

If an alpha male is the man you want to share your life with, be sure he is a man you respect. These men both want and need your respect.

Without respect, a relationship with this type of man isn't going to work. You'll have a tendency to criticize him and over time, he'll resent you for this, which is not conducive to creating the amazing relationship you're looking for.

You'll want to discover whether you share similar values. To have a good relationship, he needs to share the values that are important to you.

Below you'll find a list of 154 values. Think about which ones are important to you in men you'd be interested in dating. This is one more piece to the puzzle of helping you decide whether or not a man is right for you.

Don't over analyze. Go with your gut instinct. When you are done, narrow your list down to the top 10-15 values that mean the most to you.

---

1. Accomplished
2. Accountability
3. Activeness
4. Adaptability
5. Adventure
6. Affectionate
7. Ambition
8. Appreciative
9. Artsy
10. Assertiveness
11. Attentiveness
12. Attractive
13. Availability
14. Balanced

15. Being the best
16. Bravery
17. Calmness
18. Capability
19. Charming
20. Cheerful
21. Cleanliness
22. Cleverness
23. Comforting
24. Commitment
25. Communicator
26. Compassion
27. Confidence
28. Consistent
29. Control
30. Cooperative
31. Courage
32. Courtesy
33. Creativity
34. Credible
35. Cunning
36. Curiosity
37. Daring
38. Decisiveness
39. Delighted with life
40. Dependability
41. Depth
42. Dignity
43. Disciplined
44. Dominance
45. Dynamic
46. Educated
47. Empathy
48. Energy
49. Environmentalist
50. Ethics

51. Extrovert
52. Family
53. Fashion
54. Fearlessness
55. Fidelity
56. Financial independence
57. Fitness
58. Flexibility
59. Friendship
60. Frugality
61. Fun
62. Generosity
63. Happy
64. Health
65. Helpfulness
66. Honesty
67. Independence
68. Individuality
69. Inquisitiveness
70. Insightfulness
71. Integrity
72. Intelligence
73. Intimacy
74. Introspection
75. Introvert
76. Intuitiveness
77. Inventiveness
78. Justice
79. Kindness
80. Leadership
81. Love
82. Loyalty
83. Making a difference
84. Marriage
85. Meekness
86. Mellowness

87. Meticulousness
88. Mindfulness
89. Modesty
90. Motivation
91. Nonconformity
92. Open-mindedness
93. Optimism
94. Order
95. Outdoors
96. Partnership
97. Patience
98. Passionate
99. Peaceful
100. Perceptiveness
101. Persuasiveness
102. Playfulness
103. Power
104. Practicality
105. Preparedness
106. Pride
107. Privacy
108. Prosperity
109. Punctuality
110. Reasonableness
111. Reliability
112. Religious
113. Reputation
114. Resilient
115. Resourceful
116. Respectful
117. Responsible
118. Sacrifice
119. Saintliness
120. Secure
121. Self-control
122. Selflessness

123. Self-reliance
124. Self-respect
125. Sensitivity
126. Sensuality
127. Sexiness
128. Shrewdness
129. Sophistication
130. Spirituality
131. Spontaneous
132. Stabile
133. Status
134. Strength
135. Successful
136. Supportive
137. Sympathetic
138. Thankfulness
139. Thoroughness
140. Thoughtfulness
141. Thrifty
142. Tidiness
143. Timeliness
144. Traditionalism
145. Tranquility
146. Trust
147. Trustworthiness
148. Understanding
149. Volunteering
150. Warm-heartedness
151. Wealth
152. Wisdom
153. Wittiness
154. Youthfulness

Being with Mr. Right should be fun for you. Hopefully he

brings a smile to your face and makes you laugh. After the intense chemistry fades, you'll want a man in your life you enjoy being with.

Some people say opposites attract, but dating is so much easier when you have a few mutual activities you can share. You'll also want activities of your own as will he. Don't give up what you love doing because you're in a relationship. He needs his own interests, you need yours and the two of you need activities you can participate in together.

If something in your life is really important to you, such as family and friends, choose a man who feels the same way about it as you do. You want a man who slips easily into your life and you into his.

I can't tell you the number of women who've shared with me how they literally changed or gave up major pieces of themselves to please the man in their life.

As a woman over 50 you want a man who can love, cherish and adore you just the way you are. If he's trying to change you, maybe he's not the right man for you.

Allow yourself some time to get to know a man, especially when he's one of the nice ones with a kind and compassionate heart. Remember there are lots of men out there to date who may be a better fit worth waiting for if this man isn't the one for you.

How To Know If You're A Compatible Match

"I am not discouraged, because every wrong attempt discarded is another step forward." ~*Thomas Edison*

Once you know he has the potential to be Mr. Right, you'll want to get clearer on exactly what makes the two of you compatible. Here are some thoughts worth considering when you think you've met the one.

Is the chemistry between the two of you the type that is hot or the type that is a slow burn? There are some men you'll meet where the chemistry is instant, hot and heavy.

It's hard to stay away from each other and it's even harder to stay out of bed. You need the constant touch and feel of his body next to yours.

By the way, this type of chemistry, although it feels good, can blind you to the red flags that are waving in your face about a man.

What you really want is the slow burn type of chemistry where you feel a nice attraction on the first date. There are times when that attraction doesn't show up until you've really gotten to know a man's personality and that's why I always recommend giving nice men who want to make you happy a second, third and fourth chance.

Hot chemistry is not sustainable but slow burn is. This is the type you want for a relationship that is going to make it over time.

Next, check in on the emotional connection the two of you have. A man desires an emotional connection with a woman who makes him feel like she's a safe haven for him to come back to at the end of the day.

Men don't talk about their feelings. They were raised to

hide them. Yet men have feelings, lots of feelings, but don't know how to let you know what they are.

In fact, when you ask a man what he is feeling rather than thinking...it's pretty scary to him.

The way a man and woman connect in a relationship is when he's the brain and you're the heart. That is how you compliment each other.

This doesn't mean you give up your intelligence. Men love and respect your intelligence. What it means is he wants to connect to your heart and the softer side of you. That's what will deepen your relationship.

A key for any good relationship is about looking for and bringing out the best in each other. When the two of you first meet, everyone is at their best. You're wearing rose-colored glasses and a man you are falling for looks great.

Then the glasses come off and suddenly what started out as a beautiful relationship starts to sour because for the first time you are seeing his flaws and they are looking pretty ugly.

This is where you can get in a rut. It's impossible to have compatibility when all you can do is focus on a man's flaws. Do you remember the "**3 to 1 Game**" I taught you back in the first chapter? This is when you reminded yourself of three fantastic qualities you loved about yourself for every negative thought you had about any part of you.

Now's the time to use this exercise except this time you're going to use it when you have negative thoughts about a man. This is how you'll be able to remind yourself of what attracted him to you in the first place.

If you don't use this exercise, you'll have a hard time focusing on what's good about him and it's possible you'll toss away a good guy for not being perfect. No one is perfect, although it's nice to think we are, isn't it?

You'll want to give compatibility some time to build. In the beginning when you feel a man must have certain qualities from your Dating Wish List, like wealth or a great job, it doesn't mean you are compatible. It just means you want a man to be a certain way.

Being compatible also doesn't mean having everything in common. Compatibility is a process you will create together as you build your relationship. It's a way of life as you learn how you interact with each other and how you manage your differences when they come up.

Compatibility is something you won't be able to figure out on the first date. Over time, you'll be able to tell whether there are enough common threads bringing you together and whether you can build the relationship you desire with this wonderful man you've found.

The 3 Types Of Men You Don't Want To Date!

"If you are not being treated with the love and respect you deserve, check your 'Price Tag.'
Perhaps you've marked yourself down.
It's 'You' that determines what your worth is by what you

*accept. Get off the Clearance Rack' and get behind the
glass case where 'Valuables' are kept.
Bottom line... 'Value' yourself more."
~Author Unknown*

As you're getting the clear vision of the man you'd like in your life, I want you to be aware of three types of men that you want to stay away from.

The first is the Busy Man. He'll make plans and then change them at the last minute leaving you all alone to fend for yourself. Or he's busy with work or his family so he can't commit to making plans with you more than a few days in advance.

He loves spontaneity and you'll have "the best time" when he comes through for you this way. Your fun dates will create a false sense of hope making you think his priorities are changing. They aren't!

You'll never be able to consistently rely on this man and you'll always be at the bottom of his totem pole – never being a true priority for him. You want a man that puts you and your relationship in the first or second spot on his list. If he can't find consistent time for you now, how will he ever find the time to plan a future with you?

The next man is what I like to call The Depositor. This is the man who calls you nightly before he goes to sleep. He loves talking with you but never makes plans for getting together in person.

As you now know, men love connecting with women on an emotional level and that's what this man is doing without having to commit to you in anyway.

He'll call you nightly telling you how much you mean to

him and how he can't share his thoughts and feelings this way with anyone else in his life.

When he's done giving you his daily details, he'll apologize for monopolizing the conversation then ask you how your day went. That's when you'll hear the soft snoring begin because he's released his day to you and now he can rest peacefully. Sounds like another *activity*, doesn't it?

If this man wanted a real relationship, he'd make time for you during the day and he'd make plans to see you in person. Let another woman have this job – you deserve a man who wants to have a real physical and emotional presence in your life.

The last man you want to avoid is The Man Child. He pouts or gets huffy when you don't drop everything to hang out with him. He doesn't recognize you have your own life as well as the one you've created together.

Given half a chance, he'd figure out a way for the two of you to be joined at the hip constantly. He'd never leave your side except to go to work, then he'd run right home wanting to do an activity only with you.

Being desired by a man this way is so rare that it feels great in the beginning but over time it becomes wearing to have someone in your life who has no life without you. You'll discover he's a man who's clingy and needy.

Watch out for the man who is out there trying to fill up your calendar everyday. If you're dating this type of man, stop now! Don't allow yourself to settle just because you want a man in your life.

Men like this will only take from you, giving very little back. You deserve to have a grown up man who realizes the importance of giving you both the space and the room to enjoy the life you each brought with you into the relationship.

How To Know When You're Settling

"The minute you settle for less than you deserve, you get even less than you settled for." ~Maureen Dowd

Ever have this thought? I love this man because he'd do anything for me! When a guy is willing to do anything for you, it's pretty heady stuff making it hard to move away from him.

The problem is – if you don't love him for more than what he does for you then you are marking time.

You deserve to feel happily in love and in relationship with a man you enjoy being with on all levels. If you're not feeling it, maybe you need to go back and look at why you were attracted to him in the first place. Was it his looks, his money or maybe his emotional side? Can you find the spark again?

If not, no matter how much he does for you and how good that might feel right now, in the long run, you will be miserable dating a man who's not working for you in all ways – mind, body and soul.

Have you ever felt like this?
I don't care who it is! I just want a man in my life!

Some women will take any man they can get, just to have someone in their life to share dinner with or take to a wedding. What they often end up with is a "Project Man," a man who is needy and wants someone taking care of him emotionally and financially.

You come out on the short end of this stick, giving far more than you are getting just so you won't be lonely. You can be happy and have a great life when you're single. It's something you can create with activities you love, dinners with friends and time spent with family.

Spend some time figuring out how you can be happy as a fabulous, single woman with a great life!

This way, you'll have standards for yourself about who you will and won't date. At this time in your life, you deserve far better than a "Project Man" hanging around siphoning off the best of who you are.

Have you ever thought maybe...I'll date a man 'till someone better shows up! It's been said that what we focus on is what we get in life. You aren't leaving space in your world for the person you really want to show up if you're emotionally and physically involved and intertwined in a deep relationship with a man you're not too crazy about.

All your energy is going to a place you don't want to

be. It's actually better to be alone, date for fun or head out with your girlfriends than to mark serious time with someone you don't care that much about.

If you aren't happy with the man you're dating, be honest with him and yourself. Tell him you'd like to date other men. Or consider letting him go so you can both find partners who are better suited for each of you. You deserve a man you can love who can love you back the way you want to be loved!

Overcoming The Fear Of Relationship Failure

"Nothing hurts more than realizing he meant everything to you, but you meant nothing to him."
~ Lifelovequotesandsayings.com

David and Vicky had been going out for six months. She thought he was a great guy and enjoyed the time they spent together. He was good to her, taking her out for nice dinners, introducing her to his family and friends and even bringing her flowers on the monthly anniversary of the day they met.

David shared his feelings with Vicky, telling her he loved her. She loved him but wasn't sure she wanted to spend the rest of her life with him. She was scared the bloom would fall off the rose like it did in her 30-year marriage.

That would mean she'd be right back where she was before she started dating David…. sad, alone and lonely.

On one hand, Vicky considered cutting David loose to spend time just healing herself. On the other, she thought it might be nice to continue dating David to see where things might go.

Vicky felt silly with the whole dilemma, thinking so many women would give anything to have such a great man in their life. A part of her felt like she had messed up her marriage so much that maybe she didn't deserve a second chance with such a wonderful man.

Vicky had strong, emotional feelings about this man but was fearful of setting both herself and David up in a relationship she worried might fail like her marriage had.

Vicky was comparing two totally different relationships. While her first marriage did last for 30 years, it began when she was young. She remembered it being pretty good in the beginning.

Then the cycles of life came in and that's when changes in the relationship started to happen… They'd had children, busy careers, aging parents and eventually the empty nest happened leaving both of them feeling scared and vulnerable.

This is usually a point where men and women evaluate their lives, wondering whether the grass might be greener elsewhere. Vicky's husband felt this was the case and he'd left Vicky for another woman, leaving her feeling sad and lonely as a woman over 50. She was so afraid this would happen again with David.

I do believe partners come in our lives to help us heal our past and Vicky's been given a second chance here with a lovely man who loves her and treats her well. And she loves him.

When a relationship feels good, give it a chance. Work at setting your fears aside and see where it goes. If the fear is too strong to work out on your own, consider working with a therapist who can help you overcome any remaining fears of repeating the same mistakes over again.

A new relationship can be a wonderful gift that gives you the power to create a different type of partnership from the one you had with an ex if you are willing to give it a chance.

Summarizing the Path To Finding Your Dream Mate

*"For it was not into my ear you whispered, but into my heart.
It was not my lips you kissed, but my soul."*
~Love quotes for her

It's time to stop making excuses about the reasons you're not dating!

Do you tell yourself and everyone around you that as a woman over 50, *now* just isn't a good time in your life to date? If so, you're likely to be alone for a long time.

Just like you schedule important meetings for work, you want to schedule your dating life as well. Start by finding about 20 to 30 minutes a day to spend either online or in the real world meeting men.

Decide why you're dating!

Would you like a male friend to take to events or to watch a movie and have dinner with from time to time so you don't have to always go by yourself? Or do you desire a boyfriend or husband to share your life with? Or would you just like a sex partner for when your hormones are acting up? You need to know why you're dating so you know what type of man and relationship you are looking for.

Be realistic about men.

Are you looking for the cutest and coolest guy out there to be your boyfriend just like you did in high school? We've all aged, so cute is probably not the same as it was back then.

Yet literally overnight, a man can go from average to handsome as you bond with him. So give *average Joe* a chance when you can. He is more likely to make a better boyfriend than *Mr. Hottie* will any day.

Be visible in the world so men can find you.

Do you stay at home every night with your cat or dog watching TV? If so, you're not going to meet a lot of men. Unfortunately, men don't fall out of the sky onto your doorstep, although it would be nice if they did.

There's no time better than right now to get out there and start looking for activities in your area or dating sites that involve the type of men you'd be interested in. Check out Meetup.com. A lot of men and women our age participate in their events, especially the organized happy hours that are happening around your city.

Flirt and have fun!

It's probably been a long time since you've flirted so it may take some practice on your part to do it well again. Start by smiling at every man you see. Most will smile back at you. Whether online or on a date, be playful. Use the type of conversation and flirty behavior you'd use at a cocktail party.

Commit to going after your dream man!

Dating can feel really hard. When you find yourself rejected by a guy you really like or you feel like you've seen every man there is to see online, you may want to quit. Don't give up! Keep at it and do what it takes to find your Mr. Right.

Get dating help and support when you need it.

Women quit dating and miss out on meeting the man they're meant to be with because they just don't have the skills and techniques to deal with the dating challenges that come up. When you think about it, we weren't taught how to date back in our youth.

In fact, most of us just sort of fell into relationships and ended up marrying our high school or college sweethearts. Don't be embarrassed about getting help if you are struggling in the dating arena. It's important you have the tools and skills that will make your dating journey so much easier for you.

I can help you if you are committed to making this dream come true. Just drop me a note at **Lisa@findaqualityman.com**. We'll talk about your particular situation and how we can help you find a great guy to share your life with.

"Ask and you will receive. Seek and you will find; knock and it will be opened to you." ~Matthew 7:7

Step 5... Your Dating Blueprint

The How, When And Where For Finding Your Mr. Right!

Dating Approaches For Finding Quality Men In Real Life After 50

"When someone undermines your dreams, predicts your doom, or criticizes you in any way, remember, they're telling you their story, not yours." ~Author Unknown

Finding men to date starts with putting yourself in places and situations where available men can find you on a daily basis!

Men can't find you if you're hiding at home every night snuggled up with Fluffy or Fido reading your favorite book or watching your favorite TV shows.

You need exposure to men, whether in person or online, but unless you're getting out into the world on a regular basis, men won't know you're available.

Start going out at night and on the weekends. Consider taking classes one or two nights a week where you think there are men who might have similar interests to what you like doing.

Try learning Bridge or take some golf lessons. Men love practicing their golf swing year round and can easily be found at both indoor and outdoor driving ranges. Even the library has single men coming in to check out books.

Make a list of as many local places as you can think of where a man might be. I think you'll notice available men are everywhere. You just have to get yourself out in public areas so you have a chance of meeting one!

I want to ask you whether your vision is really narrow when it comes to the kind of men you're willing to date? When I ask women what they want in a man, the most common answer is a type similar to Richard Gere's character in *Pretty Woman*. He's rich, sassy and has a heart.

We've been spoon-fed stories like these for most of our lives, either in movies or as part of the fairytales we read as little girls. Sadly, it's jaded us to who a great guy might be, giving us unrealistic expectations of who Quality Men really are.

Stay open to dating all kinds of men with all kinds of looks, backgrounds, and interests as long as they are economically self-sufficient – meaning they can hold their own and won't be financially dependent on you.

Yes, it would be nice to have a handsome, rich man sweep you off your feet but most of the guys who look like Richard Gere are the bad boys we talked about earlier. Is that who you really want as a long time partner?

It's important you don't give up on dating after a bad date!

There is no doubt about it, without the right skill set and support in place, dating can be hard. It's so easy to get bogged down by all the profiles you see online. And having friends with no one to fix you up with can be so disheartening and frustrating that you just give up on dating.

Dating has a learning curve just like every new endeavor does. It requires learning a whole new set of skills. The more experience you get with dating, the more you will know about the type of man you really want in your life.

So when a date goes bad, chalk it up to being one man closer to the real man you're looking for.

Are You Over 50 But Dating Like You're 20?

"The best kinds of relationships begin unexpectedly. When you get the astonished feeling and everything happens so suddenly. That's why you don't look for love. It comes to you just at the right time; the time you never thought it would have."

~Author Unknown

Do you feel like it was only yesterday that you were 18 and in college? In fact, are you still wearing jeans, just more expensive ones than the ones you wore in your youth?

Unlike your mother who probably cut her hair when she married, do you still have hair that's long? And with vibrant memories of your college years still floating around, do you even feel or look like you're in your 50's or 60's or 70's?

We're all older, yet most of us – male and female alike – are still looking for members of the opposite sex the same way we did when we were in our teens and 20's.

Do you find yourself going online or out into the real world looking for that handsome, youthful man only to discover he's hard to find?

You end up seeing men who look just like your grandfather did with grey thinning hair, a belly and a boatload of baggage. It's shocking and it makes you start to think no one's out there to date – they're all too old for you!

A couple of years ago, I saw a picture on Facebook of my high school sweetheart. I remember being stunned by how old he looked. The handsome man I remembered had long black hair and still tucked away in my memory, wore painter's pants.

Over the years, when I'd imagined him aging, I just pictured an older version of the young man I went to high school with. That's probably why I was so surprised when I saw his picture.

Although still handsome, he looked like his father with snow-white hair and a suit. I remember thinking, *do I look that old too?* Somewhere deep inside, I know I do. I just don't see it when I look in the mirror. None of us do.

I was teaching a dating class in my local area and a man

came up to speak with me after class. He wanted to share his story about posting an online picture.

His daughter had volunteered to help him create an online profile. After looking through scads of pictures, he chose one of his favorites only to hear her say, "Dad, why are you posting one that's a decade old? It doesn't even look like you."

He confided in me that the picture was how he still thought of himself. He didn't realize his face had aged since it was taken.

None of us like to think we look older, but we do. As do the men we're looking to date. There are men who are still quite handsome who have aged well and there are some who haven't faired quite so well.

Yet the man with the thinning hair might be that wonderful, loving man you've been looking for, who will love you, cherish you, be your best friend and your biggest supporter. Do yourself a favor and give him the chance to impress you even if he's not the most handsome man out there.

Dating To Date Versus Dating To Mate

"A person's actions will tell you everything you need to know."
~Author Unknown

Is your dating style one of **Dating to Date** or is it **Dating to Mate**? There's a big difference between the two and one is far more fun and enjoyable than the other.

When you go on a first date, do you find yourself checking out a man's dating resume? As in, his relationship history, his job, and the kind of house he lives in?

If he has even one flaw, do you knock him out of the game right away? If so, this might be the **biggest reason** dating has become so frustrating for you and why you feel there are no good men out there worth dating.

John Grey, who wrote *Men Are From Mars and Women Are From Venus,* uses this wonderful analogy that also applies to the world of dating.

Imagine the times you've gone to a friend's house for dinner. You look around and think, *wow, what a wonderful house.* Yet, if you were planning on buying the same house, you would start hunting for its flaws, totally oblivious to its beauty and what it has to offer.

Well, when you date to mate, it's like buying the house. Your first date is spent figuring out whether he's the one you want to spend the rest of your life with. Instead of seeing his good qualities all you can see are his flaws.

Like your friend's house that's fun to visit and experience, dating to date allows you to enjoy the company of a man in the moment. His companionship provides you with a male friend, possibly a lover or even your future boyfriend or husband to share movies, dinner or maybe even a vacation.

The biggest advantage the Date to Date approach has over the Date to Mate one is the date is about having fun and enjoying each other's company. You'll be able to stop trying to figure out if he's the one like you may have done in the past.

My clients tell me over and over again how freeing this

dating style has been for them and it can be for you too! It's your first line of defense in making dating fun and easier for you!

How To Approach Quality Men In Real Life

"If not now, when?" ~*Eckhart Tolle*

You see an attractive man at your favorite coffee shop and you want him to notice you, but how do you go about making this happen?

You'll want to encourage him by giving him a signal that lets him know you're interested. This signal is what allows him to know it's safe to approach you.

You can do this by making eye contact and then you'll want to smile at him for five seconds. Yes, FIVE FULL SECONDS! It will seem like an eternity but it's a great signal for letting him know you're interested.

You can also get a man's attention by asking him a question. Remember, a man's DNA is wired to help a woman.

Here are some examples of questions you can ask that will help you get something going between the two of you.

Example #1

You're at a happy hour with a friend and a man sits down next to you. He orders red wine. Tell him you're a red wine lover but aren't sure which one to order. Ask him, "Any suggestions?" Then smile and wait for his answer.

Men love helping you and questions like these get the conversation going. The key to continuing it is to be playful. Tell him you love red wines that are spicy (which by the way are the Zinfandels). Then ask if he's into spice too.

I know it sounds odd, but serious conversation puts you in the friend zone. If your objective is to give him the signal you're interested then you want to be playful and fun. This is what will intrigue him about you.

Example #2

You're at the dog park with your dog. You see a cute guy with his dog. Go up to him and say, "Wow, that is one healthy and handsome dog, who's your vet and what's he doing to keep that dog looking so good?"

Or you can say, "Wow, that is one healthy and handsome dog, what do you feed him?" And if you have the nerve to go even further out of your comfort zone, then try this, "That is one healthy and handsome dog, just like his owner. What do the two of you do to stay so fit and strong?"

Asking questions in a flirtatious way takes practice. The first few times you may totally goof it up but don't stop trying. Every time you try it, you'll get better at knowing what to say and how to say it.

If a man doesn't respond, don't take it to heart. He may not feel an attraction to you. Or he may be married. Or he may be having a bad day. Just keep having fun asking men questions. It's a real door opener that shows a man you're interested.

Deciphering The Male Language

It's imperative to listen to what a man is really saying to you when he speaks. Men speak a language of their own that keeps them safe. It's a code that women don't always hear or understand.

Heidi was sitting at a bar having dinner with her friend. They struck up a conversation with a man who'd sat down next to them. Her friend asked the initial question that got the ball rolling and from that point on the three of them began a lively conversation.

When Heidi's friend left, she and this attractive man continued talking. He told her he was in town for a business meeting and that he lived about eight hours away. Over and over, he told Heidi he wasn't locked into where he lived and that he'd had serious relationships with women from cities other than the one he currently lived in.

She totally missed his male language hint for, *are you interested in dating me even though I live out of town?* By not listening to his words and not recognizing his signals of interest in her, she missed out on an opportunity to date a man she was very attracted to.

Love And The Handkerchief

To this day, one of my favorite television shows is *I Love Lucy*. In one particular episode, Lucy, dresses in a disguise, pretending to be another woman. She wants to see if Ricky will flirt with her. The two are walking towards each other on the street, she drops her handkerchief at his feet and says, "Pardon me," fully expecting him to pick it up for her.

Both understood this was *a signal* that meant she was interested in him and he could approach her if the attraction was mutual. You can do the same thing with men today.

In the 21st century, you can drop your phone if it's in a shatterproof case or drop a folder or package you might be carrying to get things rolling. One thing I don't recommend dropping is your purse. Men are pretty intimidated by the possibilities inside them.

It's your job to let a man know you're interested in having him approach you. His job is to ask you out if he's attracted to you and interested in pursuing you.

One last thing, if he doesn't pursue you even if you do have a great conversation and a lot of fun, just move on and chalk the experience up to another opportunity for practicing your flirting skills.

10 Ways to Tell If He's A Good Guy Or A Jerk

"We don't devote enough scientific research to finding a cure for jerks." ~Bill Watterson

1. A Jerk's Actions Don't Match His Words

A good guy will always follow through on what he tells you. When he can't, he'll let you know and won't leave you trying to figure out what happened. If he's not doing this, he's not worthy of dating you.

2. A Jerk Disappears Then Comes Back Then Disappears Again

This is a man hunting for what I call Shiny Penny Syndrome. He's looking for someone who he perceives might be a better fit than you are. What makes him a jerk is when it doesn't work out, he comes back to you until he finds his next conquest.

3. A Jerk Is A Narcissist Who Wants His Way In Every Situation

He'll manipulate you into doing what he wants to do even when you say NO. When you give in, you end up feeling like you betrayed yourself. A good guy will honor your no's.

4. A Jerk Treats Service People Poorly

If he takes you to his favorite restaurant and his meal shows up wrong, he'll blast the poor waiter with his anger. This guy often displays road rage as well. A good guy knows things can go awry and gives someone a chance to correct it.

5. A Jerk Takes You To A Party And Leaves You At The Door To Fend For Yourself

A good guy will introduce you to the people he knows in the room and will make sure you're taken care of with food, drinks and people to talk to.

6. A Jerk Only Cares About Having His Needs Met

Your needs fall far below his on the priority list. A good guy is into pleasing you and making you happy. If he's not, let him go.

7. A Jerk Is Usually Passive Aggressive

If you're trying to work an issue out, he'll act like everything is okay. Get with other people and he'll bad mouth your decision looking for confirmation from others that he's right. A good guy will work issues out with you and even if he disagrees with the final decision, he will keep it to himself.

8. A Jerk Asks You For A Date But Doesn't Call To Confirm Whether It's Happening

You end up calling him and he holds your life up, telling you he's not sure how long his meeting is going to be. A Good Guy will make sure you have the details for your date including the time, place and when he'll pick you up. Then he shows up or calls to let you know he's running late...not the other way around.

9. A Jerk Makes All The Decisions For Both Of You, Thinking He Knows What's Best For You

No one knows you better than you and a Good Guy will make sure your feelings and thoughts are part of the decision process.

10. A Jerk Doesn't Make Sure You Feel Emotionally, Physically Or Spiritually Safe

You may feel financially safe with him but that's not enough. He'll be the one criticizing what you wear or how you do things. A Good Guy may offer constructive criticism but does so in a loving way that encourages your personal growth.

The Top 15 Places For Meeting Quality

Men

"Whatever relationships you have attracted in your life at this moment, are precisely the ones you need in your life at this moment. There is hidden meaning behind all events, and this hidden meaning is serving your own evolution."
~Deepak Chopra

So where are these men you'd be interested in dating? I've come up with 15 great places worth checking out. Just remember, it's your job to get a man to notice you. So smile, ask questions or drop something if you have to.

1. The grocery store is a great place to meet men. They have to eat and unless their mom still cooks for them, they have to buy food around dinnertime. A bonus – maybe you'll find one that will cook for you, too!

2. A man is seated next to you in a restaurant – ask him what he's eating that looks so good.

3. Wine shops often have classes and tastings, which are easy to do alone. Just don't drive home inebriated or in the care of someone you don't know.

4. Dog parks – borrow a dog if you have to. Dog people are really friendly!

5. As you travel on public transportation in your city, instead of reading your book, browse around for potential suitors. Make eye contact and smile at them.

6. In a coffee shop, strike up a conversation about how long the line is or how crazy the weather has been lately.

7. Singles cruises can be fun. Just be sure you check out the average age of the passengers. And look for cruise lines that are geared more to catering to the need of men and women over 50 like Celebrity, Princess and Holland America.

8. Meet-up.com has all kinds of activities going on everyday. You can meet men interested in the same types of things you like to do. It's also a great place to meet other single women who you can make weekend plans with when you don't have a date.

9. Your hair salon – you can laugh at this, but men come in for haircuts and even manicures! I can't tell you the number of times I've sat next to a man getting a pedicure, minus the colorful polish.

10. Home improvement stores like Home Depot or Lowe's, especially on the weekend. This is a male mecca since men have to go somewhere to buy the materials they need for fixing things around their homes. Go up to men in any aisle and ask for their help when it comes to the best tools and supplies to complete your particular project. These types of situations are the key to a man's heart. He gets to be your hero!

11. Resorts – yes, men need vacations too and do travel alone. I know a woman traveling alone who met a wonderful quality man at a resort. Just be safe if you decide to have a sexual relationship.

12. Upscale casinos are popping up everywhere and men do love gambling. Hang out near the roulette table and be his lucky charm. Sit at the bar with a friend and start talking with men who come in for a drink or dinner. At the very least, play into his DNA for helping a *damsel in distress* by asking him for gambling tips.

13. Major or minor league sporting events – whew, you can just feel the testosterone in those stadiums. Make him your hero by getting him to explain what just happened in the game.

14. Places that have live music on the weekends. Men will often go have a drink at the bar while listening to the group that is playing. Best music bets for men are jazz, blues and good ole' rock and roll.

15. The very best place to meet men is an **online dating site**. Men are there 24 hours a day, 7 days a week. With patience and the right tools and skills, you can find good Quality Men on there to date.

Now it's your turn. Start writing a list of places in your area to meet new men. I think once you focus on it, you'll find available men are everywhere.

Are You Making These Dating Mistakes?

"I don't make mistakes. I date them." ~Iliketoquote.com

So you're ready to date. You've gotten your confidence into gear, you're recognizing that it's important to date like you're 50, not 20, and you're giving all kinds of men a chance.

But things aren't going well. What's happening? See if one of these **dating mistakes** could be holding you back from the man of your dreams.

"Yeah, I made mistakes but life doesn't come with instructions." ~Author Unknown

Giving off the vibe you need a man to complete your life.

It's pretty common to want a boyfriend when you're single. The world is filled with couples and it gets tiring always being the third wheel. You might be feeling sad and lonesome, sitting on the sidelines. As you watch couples hold hands and kiss, it feels like everyone but you has someone special in their life.

So you start pining for a man to come into your life. When it doesn't happen right away you begin feeling this sense of desperation. And you begin thinking if you aren't with a man, you just can't be happy.

"You cannot be lonely if you like the person you're alone with."
~Dr. Wayne Dyer

When a suitable catch shows up, you latch onto him. Next thing you know, you start texting, and emailing him constantly. You might even send sweet e-cards or worse, offer to do his laundry or run his errands so he'll think you are just *the best catch ever.*

If you find yourself doing this type of behavior, it's time to stop it right now!

Men smell desperation and it scares them. They don't want to be your "everything." That's too hard a role for anyone to live up to.

Instead of hunting for a man just to have one in your life, think about creating an exciting life of your own. When you fill yourself up with this new inner happiness, you'll no longer feel desperate for a man to do this job for you.

Dating men who don't want to be in a relationship.

Men are super honest about what they want relationship-wise. If they say they want to be part of a couple, they mean it. If they say, "I'm only looking for fun," they mean this too.

If a man tells you he wants to date around, believe him. You may be the best thing that ever happened to him but if he's convinced he wants to play the field, YOU AREN'T GOING TO CHANGE HIS MIND! Let him go and move on if his goals aren't a match to yours!

Believing there's only ONE true soul mate out there for you.

The myth: There is only one true love for you and you have to find him or you'll be miserable.

The truth: There are lots of good men out there for you to find love with. Dating is about trying different men out until you find the one that fits you best in your life today.

It's not like the story of Cinderella where the shoe only fit one person. If you choose to hold onto the belief there is only one man for you, you could end up missing all the other great men who could have so much to offer you.

How do you go about finding these great men when no one seems to be out there to date? You try the next step...

out of the box dating.

How Out Of The Box Dating Can Be Your Best Dating Friend

"As I look back on my life, I realize that every time I thought I was being rejected from something good, I was actually being re-directed to SOMETHING BETTER." ~Steve Maraboli

I'd Like Tall, Dark, Handsome And Rich Please!

Do you view men the same way you would a take out order at your local fast food joint? You know how you pull up to the Wendy's™ drive through and you ask for your single hamburger with lettuce, cheese, pickle and ketchup? You love doing this because you get exactly what you want and it's so satisfying!

Are you this way with men too? Do you want a man of a certain height? Build? Weight? Look? Particular profession? Or maybe he must have a certain amount of wealth to his name?

Does any of this sound like the criteria you may have been using in the past to attract Quality Men into your life?

I remember when I first started dating in my 40's... I was reading a man's profile that said, "I'd like a blonde, petite, professional woman who dresses well." I thought, "*Wow, this man thinks his computer can just spit out a woman made to his specifications!* "

I was bummed because he was so cute and I really wanted him to notice me. Well, he wasn't going to – I'm not blonde, nor am I petite. But what I do remember thinking is this man is missing out on a lot of great women by being so narrow with his ideas of what makes a quality woman for him.

We all get a picture in our head of who we think will make us happy. I want to fill you in on a big secret, those pictures in your head can be deceiving.

With so many expectations of who a Quality Man needs to be, you end up narrowing the number of men available to go out with you and that's what starts the mind set of *there are no good men out there to date.*

There are great men online. It may take a while to find them but they are there if you are willing to try out different types of men than you're used to dating.

It's always a good idea to come up with a list of what you'd like in a man. Although I must warn you, I made lists over the years and got men with almost 90 percent of the qualities I'd asked for.

Yet the relationships failed. Why? Because what I thought I wanted and the type of men I felt safest with were not the best men for me.

So what I want you to do is make your list of the qualities you desire in a man. Once this is done, consider changing one quality on it and start looking for men with that different quality.

It may not feel comfortable at first, because change is hard. It really is. But the benefits might be so worth it. What could happen is:

1. You will open the doors to more Quality Men who are available to date

2. You will find there are a lot of great men out there you were never aware of before and

3. You might find this different type of man is a lot of fun and far better for you relationship-wise than the men of your past.

The Top 20 Dating Strategies For Finding Mr. Right

"The best date is to be with someone who can take you anywhere without touching anything but only your heart."

~Author Unknown

1. Write a Dating Mission Statement about why you are dating and what type of relationship you hope to find with a man.

2. Be committed to dating, meaning spend time daily looking for your Mr. Right, whether online or in the real world.

3. Stop making excuses for not dating and just get out there and try it!

4. Realize limiting your beliefs about the men you must date can hold you back from finding the great guy out there who is waiting for you to find him.

5. Know the difference between what Hollywood teaches you about finding love and reality. Hollywood's version doesn't exist!

6. Don't be so perfectionistic about men that you miss the good ones. We all have flaws.

7. Figure out your Deal Breakers and only take men off your list of possibilities when they possess Deal Breaker qualities. Otherwise, give guys a first and second chance.

8. Get out of your comfort zone by flirting and dating men who are different than your usual type.

9. You are extraordinary! Show your best side when you date following the steps we discussed in Chapter 1 about getting yourself ready for dating.

10. Whether you think you can or you think you can't, you're right! Henry Ford said this about developing cars. It's true for every aspect of your life including finding good men and dating.

11. Don't come down with Shiny Penny Syndrome, thinking there is always someone better out there for you. You might miss great guys and good relationships this way.

12. Never be married to an idea of who a man must be.

13. Know the current dating rules that will make you successful at finding love again after 50.

14. Don't be too transparent on a first date by revealing all the good, the bad and the ugly about yourself. There's a time and a place for everything.

15. Go from invisibility to **rock star visibility** with a great picture and profile online!

16. Be Teflon-coated by knowing some men will like you and some won't. Let it slide off you. Sometimes it takes kissing a few frogs along the way in order to find your prince.

17. Think of every date as a learning experience and a chance to meet someone new and interesting.

18. Be courageous and go after your dating dreams.

19. Have a dating strategy in place for finding the man of your dreams.

20. Be willing to get dating help and support from friends, family, or a dating coach who will be there to help you make your dating journey a success!

Step 6... Online Dating

And How It's The Best Thing Since Sliced Bread For Meeting Quality Men At Our Age!

LISA COPELAND

Why Online Dating Is The Best Place For Meeting Men Over 50!

"Every girl deserves a guy that could make her smile even when she doesn't want to." ~Author Unknown

This may come as a shocker, but I enjoyed online dating! I dated this way off and on for almost ten years meeting some really good men I might not have met any other way. The wonderful man I'm with today who is amazing, I met at an online dating site.

When I first started dating, I had traveling to an exotic country on my bucket list. So I met a man in Australia while I was there. It didn't work out but I had quite the adventure. Dating this way for ten years has been a lot of fun for me and it can be for you, too!

I have met some really nice men online – many of whom I am still friends with today!

To be honest, unless your friends know a lot of single men to fix you up with, online dating is the best and easiest way to meet men. There is a whole *smorgasbord* of men out there on a lot of dating sites and best of all you get to choose which ones feel right for you.

Going through profiles of men is a little like walking through a huge shoe store where tons of interesting shoes line the racks. You know what it's like to wander up and down those aisles looking for the right pair of shoes? You visualize yourself in a pair you like and then you think about how it might work with your current wardrobe.

Next you try them on and some you absolutely love so you buy them because they fit you perfectly and make you feel great about yourself. Some you just like and those shoes, you may or may not buy. Some you put back on the shelf because they don't fit or they look funny on your feet.

**Online dating is a lot like one of those shoe stores!
You have a wonderful opportunity here to choose from a
wide variety of men.**

When I first started dating in 2002, online dating wasn't as common or accepted as it is today. Today, online dating is considered to be mainstream. When you stop and think about it, where else can you meet so many single men over 50 in one place?

With a positive attitude of *I'm going to just have fun*, along with the right skills – many of which you're learning in this book – you could end up meeting your Mr. Right like I did and like so many of my clients have! The system does work!

How The Right Profile Gets The Right Men To Notice You

"Real Men don't love the most beautiful girl in the world. They love the girl who can make their world the most beautiful."

~www.goodmorningwishes.com

Online dating is tricky and although it takes some work to find the man you want, it can be a fantastic way to meet single, available men over 50. From this moment on, I'd like you to think of online dating as a **"Virtual Cocktail Party."**

Imagine yourself at a real cocktail party, talking with a man you just met. You'd put your best self forward, intriguing a man by being flirty and fun. A profile needs to be the same way.

To get a man's attention, you'll want a profile that showcases the best YOU!

Profile Pictures That Are Turn Offs To Men

• Don't wear clothing that reveals too much. A little cleavage is acceptable but showing three quarters of your breast covered only by a small piece of material is not. They think you are looking for a sex partner.

• DON'T post pictures where a man needs a magnifying glass to see you. I don't care how beautiful that mountain is behind you. If it takes up more space than you do, then don't use the picture.

• DON'T post pictures with your friends. How many times have you looked at pictures men have posted with friends, wondering which one is the guy who wrote the profile? And how often did you wish he were they guy's friend posting the profile because he was hotter? Men do the same thing when you post pictures with other women. Do yourself a favor and only post pictures of you!

• DON'T post pictures with other men, even if he is your son, brother or father. Believe it or not, men think it's someone you've dated in the past and it turns them off to see you with another man.

• DON'T take SELFIES. No one likes seeing someone's toilet or the camera covering half your face in the mirror.

Profile Pictures Men Love!

• You DO want to take a picture that shows your best assets. If it's your legs, be sure to show them. If it's your waist, show that. You want to grab a man's attention with what is great about you.

• DO you know that you have ten seconds to get a man's attention? Make your picture count!

• DO post at least two great pictures of you; a good headshot and a full body shot. When you only post headshots, men think you are hiding something you don't want them to see. And often that's exactly what you're doing. I know you're probably figuring once they get to know you, it won't matter. Believe me, it does matter and it makes him think if you're dishonest about this, what else aren't you telling him? Be honest here because in reality, you want a guy who accepts you for exactly who you are so you may as well show him who you are upfront.

• DO hire a pro or ask a friend or one of your kids who is camera savvy to do this for you. The advantage of a professional picture is they help you stand out from everyone else on the site. Just make sure the photographer does minimal retouching.

• DO wear clothing that makes you look and feel your best. You take a better picture when you are feeling like the amazing woman you are.

• DO post recent pictures. I admit it's nice to look like you're 40 again but there's something wrong when a guy has to call you because he can't figure out which one you are at the Starbucks where you're meeting.

• DO SMILE! Men are naturally drawn to pictures of women who smile. Your smile makes you glow and gives the impression you are fun and positive to be around. This is so attractive to the men you want to meet!

Your Amazing Profile

Work at keeping the I's in your profile to a minimum. Think about it – when you go to a party and you meet someone who keeps saying, "I do this," "I like that," "I am this," don't you get bored?

Your Profile Template

- Profiles should be flirty and engaging.
- They should be no more than three short paragraphs.
- Paragraph one is about you.
- Paragraph two is about what you're looking for in a man.
- Paragraph three is a short vignette of an activity the two of you might do together that a man can visualize.
- And lastly, ask a question that invites him to write to you if he's interested.

In your third paragraph vignette, it's nice to write about romantic ideas in your profile, like sharing a bike ride or having a glass of wine together, as long as sexual innuendos are left out. This attracts the wrong type of man who will write you back, thinking a sexual partner is all you're looking for online.

Consider leaving out the words, "I'm looking for my 'soul mate' in your profile." Men have told me they see it in every woman's profile so it does nothing to catch their attention.

Your goal is to look unique, not the same as every other woman online.

A man doesn't need to know all there is to know about you in this first introduction. Save the details about your life for when the two of you meet. And even then, you don't need to put your whole life on the table. A date is about meeting someone new and interesting who might be worth considering for a second date. That's it.

The ONLY purpose of your profile is to open the door for a Quality Man to notice you and want to write you.

Try not making demands in your profile about salaries and how you'd like to be entertained at the most expensive restaurants in your area. Even guys with money don't want a woman telling them where to go and what to do.

Do represent yourself, showing who you are today. Otherwise, it's like false advertising. Pretending to be someone you're not just to attract the man you think you want is a very hard persona to keep up. You have no control over who a man ultimately wants or is looking for.

Your power comes from knowing what qualities you want in a man.

Make a promise to yourself that you will take the time to write a really good profile that is interesting and flirty, yet short and engaging that can capture a Quality Man's attention online. Add a great picture of you smiling and you'll have the winning combination for attracting the man of your dreams.

One more thing you should know is that men our age usually like being the one to make first contact online with a woman. A few relationships I know of have worked the other way around but most of the time, it will fizzle if you've made the first move.

If you're having trouble getting men to write you, take a look at your profile and see what might need some updating. Working with private clients, I've found that sometimes all it takes is a tweak or two for men to start noticing you. Maybe a new picture, or just taking out some of the lines I shared with you that turn men off. Just one change can make a huge difference in the types and quality of men you attract.

How To Get Your Kids Helping You With The Challenges Of Online Dating

"Hope for love, pray for love, wish for love, dream for love... but never put your life on hold waiting for love."
~Mandy Hale

Unlike our children, we weren't brought up with computers. So technology can be daunting at times when it comes to dating online. Your adult children can be your biggest cheerleaders when it comes to seeing you happy again and are often willing to help you navigate through the technology of dating in cyberspace.

As we discussed in Chapter 1, have your adult daughters go shopping with you for some new dating clothes and makeup that enhance your best features. What kid isn't willing to make a few suggestions about clothing that looks both fantastic and age appropriate on you.

If you don't want to hire a professional just yet to take your picture, consider getting your kids to use their smart phone to take a couple shots of you. Remember to smile and look happy!

This next task may require a glass of wine for both of you and a lot of patience as you have your adult children teach you how to navigate through all the pictures and profiles of men on dating sites. While you're at it, have them show you how to download and use mobile apps for the dating sites you're on.

It's time to upload your pictures. Most boomers are clueless on this one, so again, patience and another sip of wine will help you both get through this process. You want to learn this skill so you can add and delete pictures without your kids and a bottle of wine by your side.

Next, have your kids show you how to set up a dating email account that doesn't reveal your last name. You'll want to use this email address to communicate with men outside the site.

Many boomers still have landlines – something your children stopped using when they left home long ago. You don't want to use your home phone to speak with a new man. Caller ID gives out way too much information about you.

Instead you'll give a man your cell number but before you do, have your kids help you hide the Caller ID information. This may require a call to your cell carrier.

Another option is getting a Google phone number. They're free and are not traceable back to you. When I began dating about six months after a relationship had ended, I figured I would give men my cell number to call me.

I gave it to the first man I went out with. Then I got back an email titled, "So you're a dating coach." He had Googled my cell number and found out what I did on the Internet instead of hearing it directly from me. The moral of the story is get a Google number so men can't learn too much about you.

Are There Good Men Even Online?

"No I am not single. I am in a long distance relationship because my boyfriend lives in the future." ~Author Unknown

Nancy had just gone on her fifth, miserable first date. Her latest dating site of choice was Chemistry.com. She'd tried quite a few dating sites, feeling like they just weren't working for her.

When she shared her story with me, she'd met a man who was 49 – the same age as her – who lived in a nearby suburb. They'd emailed a couple of times then he asked her to meet him at a fancy restaurant.

She was thrilled that he'd listed fine dining as one of his interests and she assumed his invitation meant he wanted to meet for dinner. He'd listed an income of $100,000-$150,000 and his profile said he worked as an investor. She later found out he was a slum landlord.

Nancy arrived looking quite nice in her favorite dress. He was not there yet, so she went to the ladies room to freshen up. When she got back, the hostess said he was out on the patio. Two glasses arrived shortly after she sat down.

The menus had been removed from the table and as she watched other diner's food pass by her table, she realized he must have told the waiter they were only there to have drinks.

During her date, she found out his son had moved back in with him, along with his wife and two toddlers. Then Nancy asked about his other children and found out his daughter was still living with him as well!

Her date was not very warm or caring and he appeared to be rather detached and distracted as they sipped their wine. This date is what broke the camel's back for her. It led Nancy to wonder whether there was any kind, caring men even available to women her age.

I'm sure there have been times you've wondered the same thing. I want to assure you that YES, there are lots of kind, caring men available for you to date online!

The key is figuring out who is a good match for you, as we did in Chapter 4. If you haven't done it yet, take a few minutes and jot down a list of qualities you're looking for in a Quality Man along with your deal breakers and how you want to feel around him when you're together. Now that you have your list, it's time to take it with you as you visit your favorite online dating site.

Spend some time browsing sites to see what each one has to offer. Then sign up for one or two sites that you think might work for you. Keep in mind, it usually takes more than a month to find the love of your life. And don't be afraid to use free sites. A lot of men who are on paid sites are also on OK Cupid and Plenty of Fish.

Be aware of judging a man based solely on the picture he's posted. You might find he looks so much better in person. Or as we've discussed before, you might find his personality makes him endearing when you meet – qualities you can't always see in a picture.

Dating is a numbers game, so it takes consistency to be successful. Spend at least 20 to 30 minutes daily browsing men's profiles, writing to men you are interested in and responding to emails men have sent to you.

It's a good idea to invest time speaking with a man on the phone before meeting him in person. Nancy could have learned a lot about this man by spending a few minutes chatting with him prior to their date. This is how you can avoid dates with men not worthy of your time.

Don't become a phone pal but do spend a little bit of time talking on the phone.

One to three conversations will give you a good basis for deciding whether or not you want to meet and get to know a man further.

How To Tell Who The Good Guys Are Online

"Men aren't stupid, and you don't need a complicated set of rules to find a good one who loves you. Here's the only rule you need: if a man loves you, he will do anything he can to keep you around. Anything!" ~Author Unknown

When you first hop on a dating site, it can be pretty exciting to see all those men on there looking for love just like you are. You might even feel like a kid in a candy store.

Remember the penny candies you bought as a kid? Sometimes, it was hard to make a choice because there were so many to choose from.

Like the candy store, online dating can feel overwhelming. You see all those male faces staring at you from your computer screen. You read all those profiles filled with men's hopes and dreams. You start wondering how you can sort through this sea of faces to find the men worthy of dating you.

The solution lies in using what I call Male Online Sorting Filters.

Start by having your Male Wish List and your Deal Breakers close to you so you can use them as a reference when you go online. Next, head to your favorite dating site and begin looking at men's pictures. Look for clues about his life by noticing the way he's dressed, the background surrounding him and who's in the picture with him. You can learn a lot about a man this way.

If family values are important to you and a man has a picture posted with his kids, you know family is a priority for him as well. If he displays a picture with his giant Great Dane, you know his dog plays a significant role in his life. If you're not a dog person, you know this picture is a clue for you to move on.

If you've found clues in his picture that pique your interest, then read his profile. Be sure to pay attention to the words he's written to see if they match the values and qualities you've written on your Wish List. Also this is the time to note whether he has any of your Deal Breakers.

Look for what he likes to do in life and see how compatible it is to your lifestyle. If he rides motorcycles every weekend and you're not into motorcycles, he probably isn't the best match for you. Yet if he says it's a hobby he likes to do on his own occasionally, he's a possibility.

If you like his picture and what he has to say, make him a favorite and see where it goes.

Is He Or Isn't He A Quality Man?

Elizabeth was tired of being disappointed by the men she'd met online. Men seemed so nice both in their profiles and when they'd meet. But as she would get to know a man, he'd change and she felt so unsettled by this.

She was totally frustrated and began wondering if there was some way to tell the good guys from the bad ones online.

I shared with her that when men and women first meet, both bring the best sides of themselves to the dating table. It's a little bit like a play where actors are pretending to be someone else. You do it because you want to appear wonderful so the person sitting across the table likes you.

So what happens is you find yourself falling in love with that wonderful person you think you know. But in reality, what's happening is you are falling in love with an idea of who you think this man is. Your idea does not necessarily match the reality of the man himself.

Think about it… Anyone can act a certain way for an hour, a day, even a couple of weeks or months, but no one can sustain first date behavior forever. Over time, true personalities start coming out.

You can't really tell who a man is until you've spent a fair amount of time together. But there are signs you can watch for that will help you identify the good guys from the not-so-good men out there.

A Non-Quality Man

Will be abrupt with you. Maybe he cuts you off and doesn't let you voice your opinions or maybe he totally disregards your feelings.

He's secretive, meaning he purposely avoids answering questions about different parts of his life and you know he's hiding something but can't quite put your finger on it.

He seems condescending. He is laughing at you – not with you – and telling you that you aren't enough, whether it's smart enough, pretty enough or thin enough. He makes you feel not okay about who you are.

He's often evasive, which means he'll change the subject or laugh it off, saying, "we'll talk about it later," but never does.

If you meet a man who consistently exhibits these qualities, you might want to reconsider and let him go. His behavior won't get better over time.

A Quality Man

Will be both honest and loyal, wanting to share his life with you.

He'll want to make you happy and part of this is telling you how wonderful you are and how much you mean to him. He'll walk his talk, meaning he follows through on whatever he tells you he'll do to the best of his ability. He'll want to hear about your life as well as have an active role in it.

This is a good guideline to use as you talk and meet men online. Just take it slow and be careful of getting too emotionally attached to who you think he is versus who he really is.

Why Do I Always See The Same Guys Online?

"The reason people find it so hard to be happy is that they always see the past better than it was, the present worse than it is, and the future less resolved than it will be."
~Marcel Pagnol

Having dated off and on for years, I know it's common to see some pretty familiar faces staring back at you of men who have been online forever using the same old pictures and profile.

So I wasn't surprised when I saw pictures of guys I'd dated years ago, including the one I called the "KFC Man."

"KFC Man" and I talked when I was in my 40's and just starting out on my dating journey. He told me he didn't care what a woman looked like, as long as her body was fit and toned.

Then he asked what mine was like. I was feeling insecure about being judged as not ok enough so I avoided the question. Instead, I told him I had an aide who wheeled me up to the 'KFC' counter every day for my daily dose of fried chicken. I shocked him and for a full minute he said nothing. I finally said, "Just kidding."

Ten years later, he was back online, probably because no one was able to meet his stringent expectations of who a woman should be to date him.

This time around, his profile seemed nicer. We will never know but maybe he's finally learned that a woman who has more than just a certain body type can indeed be both appealing and interesting.

I understand how frustrating online dating can be when you see unchanged profiles and the same pictures that were posted years ago. It's depressing. It makes you want to give up on dating and it makes you feel as though absolutely no one is out there to date except the same men you've seen for years.

You want to keep in mind that people do go in and out of relationships. And although it would be nice to see updated pictures, some men are lazy about updating their profiles.

Men have expressed the same frustration about women's pictures and profiles never being updated. Make sure that you update yours every time you go back online.

One way to change the pattern of seeing the same guy over and over again is to get out of your usual "dating box" by choosing a couple of new dating sites that are entirely different from the ones you're used to. You may find a small number of men who are a repeat from your favorite site. But for the most part, you should see completely different men on the new site.

Here are two great resources for finding new dating sites online that might be a better fit for you. www.findaqualityman.com/dating-sites/ and at www.100bestdatingsites.org.

The Men You'll Meet Online

"Online everyone can be who they want to be. It only gets tricky when you meet them in the real world." ~tokii.com

Thousands, if not millions, of men are on dating sites every day looking for the woman of their dreams. I've identified the most common types of men you'll find online to help you figure out which one is the right type for you.

The Needy Man

While you're still in the emailing process, he's already thinking of you as his girlfriend and starts calling you *honey* or *my girl*. He wants to talk with you on the phone or text you constantly, leaving you no space for yourself. He always wants to be at your side. If you love a good project, he's perfect for you.

The Motorcycle Dude

Lots of men ride motorcycles, including doctors, lawyers, and well-paid businessmen. You can get an idea from his pictures whether he's the kind of man you'd be interested in. Don't knock him out yet for having this midlife hobby. All you have to do is let him enjoy being an "Easy Rider" on his own. You never have to ride his motorcycle unless you want to.

Beware Of The Ring On His Finger

Usually a man who doesn't post pictures is married. He has no interest in being spotted by his wife's single friends while he hangs out on dating sites. Many will even admit they're married when they write to you, freely talking about why they're cruising dating sites in spite of it. I'd stay away from this type of man. They rarely leave their wives even after proclaiming a deep love for you. You are the one who gets hurt. He has a wife at home to go back to when things fizzle.

Flying The Friendly Skies To Date

The biggest drawback to long distance relationships is the illusion and fantasy you create based on an inordinate amount of phone time the two of you will share. When you do finally meet, the real man usually doesn't match up to the fantasy one you've created in your head.

This type of relationship is hard to do. That being said, it can be done if you live within two hours of each other and can find the time to see each other on a frequent basis. This guy works particularly well if you're looking for a weekend husband.

What He Really Needs Is A Shrink, Not A Date

He's looking for a therapist and will gladly use you for the purpose of working out his issues. Steer clear. Unless you're being paid by the hour to listen to him complain about his ex and how she's torturing him, you'll be much better off finding a man who has gotten over his last relationship.

The Take Out Order Man

These are the men who think they can order up a certain type of woman online. They act as if they are going through the drive through at Wendy's. Instead of asking for a hamburger with cheese, lettuce and pickle, they expect the site to give them a woman with a specific kind of job, body, hair color and more.

These are men looking for perfection based on their expectations of how a woman should be. You're better off sticking with men who think you're great exactly how you are! You'll never be able to please this one.

The Bad Boy

He's gorgeous! He's charming and a he's major player who will break your heart. He's always looking for where the grass might be greener. He might be fun to play with but he's not good for long-term relationships!

He may be hot but getting hurt (and you will by this one) is not worth it unless he's just another guy you want to check off your "been there done that list."

The Scammer

These are the men who've taken some of the fun out of dating. They are easy to spot when you know what to look for. We'll cover more about this in the next chapter.

Younger Men Looking For Cougars

Younger men are really into older women. It's great for the ego. Go for it if you want to experience a playmate in the sandbox!

The Older Man

Older men are "old school" gentlemen who treat you like a lady. Because they grew up with boomers, they often consider themselves part of that culture. You're likely to have more in common with these men than you will with younger men in their 30's looking for cougars.

These men will make you feel young compared to how old they are. This could be a bonus or a drawback depending on the guy. It's worth trying for sure!

The Quality Man

A "Quality Man" may not be the most handsome man online but he is the nicest and he will do anything for you. He's the man who's interested in what you're doing. He's the one who will post pictures of his children and his dog, trying to convey his good values that you might want to consider.

Lots of Quality Men are online and they want nothing more than an opportunity to love you and make you happy. All you have to do is figure out what a Quality Man means to you then use the tools you're learning here to start finding him. He's definitely worth giving a chance!

How To Identify And Avoid Online Scammers

"Fraud is the daughter of greed". ~ Jonathan Gash

Women over 50 can feel vulnerable when it comes to dating online and often worry about being taken advantage of by men who might scam them.

Recently, I heard yet another story of a woman connecting with a scammer on a legitimate dating site. These men are con artists who will find a way to touch your heart and your pocketbook without a second thought.

I don't want to scare you and cause you to stop going online. There are plenty of good men out there for you to date. But there are certain clues you need to be aware of that will tip you off to potential scammers.

The Clues In Your Profile

Don't mention your income or where you work. You can say you're a nurse or an executive but don't mention where or how much you make.

Be aware of sounding needy and lonely in your profile. It makes you perfect prey for scammers looking to hook you into their scam.

Anyone Can Create An Online Profile

Remember how quickly you set up your account at an online dating site? It really only takes an email address and maybe a credit card. Someone who wants to scam you can create ten profiles in just a few minutes using pictures that aren't their own, along with sensual words that attempt to draw you in.

Think of the dating profiles you come across as store windows. The display might look nice, but you have to go in the store and explore a little more before you buy.

A Man Living Outside the US

These men will often say they live in the country you live in but their work takes them elsewhere in the world. They tell you they'll be coming back soon…to wait for them because can't wait to meet you.

Who He Really Is

Most of these men come from Ghana, a country in Africa. It's a poor country and jobs that pay well are scarce. In a couple of hours a day, they can easily communicate with you, find your weak spot and make a fortune preying on your emotions.

They speak with British accents something American women easily fall for. It's sounds romantic to us. These men know it and use this to their advantage.

Where They Say They Are From

Usually they will tell you they were born in England to a British mother and Italian father. They give themselves romantic names like Valentino and Antonio.

They will send you pictures of themselves and they're usually drop dead gorgeous. That's because they're using pictures they've found on the Internet of handsome models.

You can tell because the men are usually posing in hats no normal man would wear, but you ignore this because you're taken by how good looking he is.

Besides hats, you'll see men wearing sunglasses while holding products like beer or wine standing in front of tall buildings in Metropolitan cities, or standing by expensive cars.

Sometimes they'll send you pictures of men with a consistent quality like brown hair or the same color eyes that just makes you think he sent pictures from different times in his life.

Scammers might even send you family pictures of wives and children or grandchildren. Rarely are they in the picture with them. This is a huge tip off.

They play on your idea of romance with poems

Women love romance and these men use this knowledge to lure you into their scheme sending you beautiful poems they've found on the Internet.

What They Talk About

As you chat for hours every day, scammers will find your weak spot. If you've lost a close member of your family, don't be surprised if they tell you they have too.

They use holes in your heart to get you to trust them. We bond easily with people who've had similar losses in their lives.

Once they've bonded with you, they will share news of the big business deal they are in. You'll hear how they just need a little more money to finish it.

They'll tell you this is all the money the bank will give and their family members have invested too. Then they'll email you copies of contracts to make the deal seem legit and ask you for a loan just until the deal is signed. They'll then share with you that once the deal is done, they'll wire your money back to your bank account.

Never, ever give them access to your financial resources. And do not wire money to anyone outside the country you live in until you've spoken with your attorney or financial advisor.

Through this negotiation you hear a lot of I love you baby...I can't wait to see you baby and as soon as this clears up I'll be there and we'll be together.

Excuses For Never Being Able To See You

They'll express how badly they want to see you. They'll even go so far as to tell you they are making arrangements to travel to where you live in the next month or two.

Yet as the date arrives, suddenly they aren't available and the date gets moved again. This is another HUGE TIP OFF you're dealing with a scammer.

You Google Them

Try Googling your Valentino or Antonio. More than likely nothing will show up. But, if you tip them off you've done this...within days you will see a listing pop up with their name and phone number.

They want you to believe they are legit. They'll even tell you they got to the bottom of the issue by speaking to the supervisor who finally corrected the huge mistake the phone company made not listing their information.

Scammers will list their jobs in the residential white pages online. This is something few legitimate businesses do.

How To Protect Yourself

Date men closer to home. Keep emails to no more than three or four. Move men to the phone and keep calls to a minimum of one or two, then meet ASAP.

If a man tells you, he'll be out of the country for a month or two, tell him to give you a call when he gets back. In the meantime, stop communicating with him. You don't want to get pulled into a fantasy relationship that will rip your heart in two and wipe you out financially if you're not careful.

He will try and keep you in the communication process as long as he can with his romantic poems and sad stories of his life.

He wants you to feel guilty saying "No" to him. He wants you to think thoughts about him like... *He's so nice...He's so cute...He's led such a difficult life...His life is such a sad story.*

Don't get pulled into this con. Move on and date other men so you're not too attached to any man until you know he's legit.

If this has happened to you, you are not alone. Thousands of men and women get caught up in these scams daily. Situations like this can leave you feeling emotionally devastated. You might find you have a hard time trusting men again.

If you'd like to work on rebuilding your dating confidence, I hope you'll write me at **lisa@findaqualityman.com**. We'll set up a time to talk about how to get started rebuilding the dating life you really want.

I want you to remember there are lots of good men out there to date online. Not every man online is a scammer.

When perusing a dating site, remember these tips I've shared with you about identifying scammers. If you're feeling uncertain about whether or not a man is scamming you, share your story with your friends. They are objective and can give you an honest opinion of what they believe is going on.

If You Want to Find Mr. Right Then Stop

Making These Online Dating Mistakes

"Simple Rules In Life:
If you do not go after what you want, you'll never have it.
If you do not ask, the answer will always be no.
If you do not step forward, you will always be in the same place."
~Author Unknown

It's a problem if you're only viewing the profiles of really good-looking men online. Everyone loves the beautiful people because – let's face it – their looks rub off on us making us look and feel better about ourselves. Just standing next to them can make you feel like your value has gone up a few notches.

What you're up against is the best looking people online are like the popular kids back in school. Everyone wants to be with them.

Just because someone is good looking doesn't mean they will make the best boyfriend, husband, or date. It just means they look REALLY good and you've placed a high value on this quality.

A lot of average looking men who might make better long-term boyfriends and future husbands get passed over daily for not looking like George Clooney.

Can you think of any men you might have met in real life that seemed average until you got to know them? As you discovered his personality, he started appearing more and more handsome to you. There are men out there who take bad pictures yet look far better in person.

Before you decide to throw an "Average Joe" away, read his profile to see if there is potential based on other qualities he might have; not just his looks.

Another mistake women make is interviewing a man on a first date. When you do, you're carrying the burden of having to figure out if this man is "the one" in 30 minutes or less.

As a woman over 50, you don't need a husband to make babies anymore. This is a time in your life where you can play and have fun with men creating any type of relationship you want. Take advantage of this.

You might not find your next boyfriend, but you could find a great guy pal that you can have fun with on weekends. It's far better than sitting at home every Saturday night watching Lifetime or Hallmark romantic movies all alone.

Finally, are you making men you meet online your email pen pal? This is the quickest way to getting nowhere fast in over 50's dating.

An email relationship is nothing more than a fantasy relationship. Information gets shared on a deeper level due to the false sense of safety and intimacy email creates. If your meet and greet doesn't work out, you might regret having revealed so much information to someone you didn't really know. It's better to limit emails to a maximum of five to seven per person.

Why Do Men Disappear Online?

"Holding a grudge is letting someone live rent free in your head."
~Author Unknown

Often, women get letters from men who seem very interested in getting to know them. They're sharing emails back and forth...then suddenly, the man disappears and communication ends.

The plain and simple truth is he's probably emailing back and forth with more than one woman at the same time he's emailing you. He ends up going on a date with someone he likes and wants to pursue and that's why he stops communicating with you.

There are two things you can do to handle situations like these in the future. Move the email and phone process to the meet and greet as soon as you can without being aggressive. And don't let yourself get emotionally invested in a man you are just emailing or spending time with on the phone.

It's a set up for dating frustration because the energy between the two of you can be totally different or non-existent in person even though it's great through technology.

Sometimes a man shows back up in your life when it doesn't work out with another woman. If he does and you're still interested, meet him quickly so he doesn't have enough time to disappear again with someone else.

To keep your sanity in dating, try not looking at men disappearing as a personal rejection of you.

Sometimes you just don't match the picture of who he thinks he wants. You can't change this. What you can do is get back online and find someone who thinks you're the greatest woman they ever met.

Why Are Men Sending Me Those Annoying Form Letters?

"You've only got three choices in life: Give up, give in, or give it all you've got." ~Author Unknown

Have you ever had a man write you a note online and when you opened it, it read just like a form letter? He says nothing personal about you. He does share his story and he suggests you write him if his letter sparks your interest.

Men send as many as 100 letters to women online and receive a response from only three. Men take a pounding in the form of rejection from women on dating sites. It's rough on their egos. To protect themselves, they stop being the nice guy who sends personal notes.

Out of sheer frustration they send this dating resume about their life to all the new women who show up on the dating sites. Their hope is one of these women will raise their hand and say, "I'm interested!"

These men want a relationship with a good woman. Even though they're doing it in a way that is a total turnoff to most women, the guy sending out the dating resume might be worth answering when a relationship is what you're looking for too!

Step 7... The Etiquette Of Dating After 50

The Secrets You Need To Find Mr. Right In The Over 50's Dating World

LISA COPELAND

Can I Email A Man?

"You come to love not by finding the perfect person, but by seeing an imperfect person perfectly." ~Sam Keel

I usually recommend you let a man contact you. It often fizzles when you're the first to get the ball rolling. Now that being said, I know of two very good relationships where the woman contacted the man first. It's worth a try if you are really interested in a man. Just make sure you aren't attached to whether or not he writes you back.

Remember, online dating is like a virtual cocktail party. You're fun, flirty and cute. You want to use your flirty, feminine energy to answer emails from men.

To do this, take a few moments to collect your thoughts before answering a man's letter. Keep your answers short and be sure to ask a fun question he can respond to.

You'll often find when questions aren't asked, the email flow ends.

If he starts asking serious questions in his emails, then suggest taking your conversation to the phone. This gives you the opportunity to screen a man to see if he's worth dating. If you choose to meet without this step, you could be quite surprised by who shows up.

Trudy had a date with a guy who emailed he'd like to meet her at a local ice cream shop. She got there and joined him at a table outside the store. They started talking and not once did he suggest they get ice cream. Why?

As they spoke further, he revealed he had no job and no money. Had Trudy spent a few minutes on the phone speaking with him, she'd have avoided wasting her time with a man she had no desire to date.

Phone conversations are about starting the process of getting to know someone better. Then you'll both have the opportunity to see if you want to take it to the next level of meeting.

There are some men who can't seem to get past the phone phase. If he doesn't ask you out by the second call, you're becoming a phone pal, not someone to explore a relationship with. Move on!

When I first started dating in my mid 40's, I had no clue what to do when it came to men and online dating. I look back and wince at how often I allowed men to make me their email pal or phone pal. In all honesty, back then, I was thrilled by this turn of events.

I figured they picked ME to talk with, so in return, it was my female duty to let them yak for hours about themselves and their day.

Night after night, I'd think I was doing the right thing… Yet guess what? No date ever came out of one of these nighttime talkers.

I had to learn the hard way how to set boundaries with these men. I don't want you to have to do the same thing.

How To Stop Being A Man's Phone Pal

"There's a difference between interest and commitment. When you're interested in doing something, you do it only when it's convenient. When you're committed to something, you accept no excuses; only results." ~Author Unknown

If you're talking with a man night after night for hours on end, you're in a phone ONLY relationship. You want to stop this immediately! Think about it… By the fifth conversation, it starts getting pretty boring. But you don't want to be thought of as rude in case he decides to ask you out.

Yet why would you want to date a guy who is only interested in sharing his daily life and has no real interest in yours? This type of relationship is not worth investing your time in.

I know it feels good to have a man who wants to speak to you at the end of the day. But this type of relationship is a dead end. If he wanted to date you, he'd have already asked you out.

He's looking for the emotional connection he can only get from a woman. And you're making it easy for him to get it by spending hours every night listening to his tales.

After two phone calls, if he hasn't asked you out, you can say something like, "I enjoy talking with you on the phone. I'd *really* enjoy putting a face to that great voice."

If he doesn't get the hint, be a little more blunt about it and sweetly say, "I've enjoyed our time talking together. I feel like it would be fun if we met and put faces to the voices and great conversations we've been having. What do you think?"

This sentence is fun and flirty and it puts a man in the position of being your hero by stepping up to doing something that would make you happy.

If he doesn't ask you out right then and there, it's time to let him go. After all, wouldn't it feel better to be in a real relationship with a man who wants to spend time with you going to the movies, taking you to dinner and giving you a long kiss and a wonderful hug at the end of your date?

Should Your First Date Be Coffee or Dinner?

"The best accessory a girl can own is her confidence." ~ *Krexy*

He sounds nice on the phone and he asks you to meet him for dinner. You might go to some nice places this way but if a date is not going well, it can be a very long meal and you have to be at your best for at least an hour or longer.

Meeting at a coffee shop can be short and sweet and you can be out of there within half an hour if he's not the guy for you. If the date is going well, you can take it to a meal but I do suggest limiting first dates to about two hours. Leave some mystery and intrigue for the next time.

Always have an exit strategy in place for when a date isn't going well.

I remember a date where I had to use an exit strategy to escape. I couldn't figure out who my date was since no one in the coffee shop looked remotely like the picture of the man I'd seen online.

I picked up my phone and called him. This is one of the reasons why you want to exchange cell numbers prior to meeting.

Whether you're running late and need to text or you can't find him at the place you agreed to meet, you'll have a way to contact him if you get his number in advance.

This man was at least one hundred pounds heavier than his picture. His pants were falling off and in his hands were a brown bag that he later told me was his medicine for his heart he'd just bought. This was strike number one – he had lied about how he looked.

He hugged me and the first words out of his mouth were, "My dog has fleas." That became strike number two, as I have a dog and just hearing this gave me the willy-nillies.

Strike number three came when we sat down and he started talking about his CPAP breathing machine. This was way too much information for a first date and now with three strikes, I was ready to leave.

Before I discovered exit strategies, not wanting to be rude, I would have stayed on a date until the guy signaled it was time to end it.

Not this time. I remember looking into my cup of tea for courage, and then I looked up at him and said, "I'm sorry. I forgot I had a 7:30 meeting when I scheduled our time together. I need to go in about 15 minutes." And I did.

The funny thing is, he had no clue it was an exit strategy because he asked me out again. I declined. Now, I'm going to give you permission to politely leave dates when they aren't going well using one of these nine exit strategies.

The only thing I urge is that you be nice, polite and respectful when you use an exit strategy. He isn't a bad guy. He's just not the one for you!

These exit strategies work best when you meet for coffee. It's pretty rude to leave in the middle of dinner but you can put one in place prior to ordering or shortly after the plates are removed from the table.

Nine Exit Strategies For When A Date Isn't For You!

1. You can always be honest and say, "I enjoyed meeting you and appreciate you buying me a drink, but this I feel this isn't working for me."
2. You can arrange ahead to have a friend call you with a made up crisis about 15 minutes into a date.
3. You can always say you have a meeting you forgot you had to go to and will have to leave shortly.
4. Talk non-stop trash about your ex. He'll think you're a drama queen but who cares? He'll high tail it out of there pretty quickly.
5. Want to scare him and get him to take a hike? Talk about how you want to be married by the end of the year. Then start asking a ton of personal questions as if you were interviewing him for the job. You come across as desperate and most guys will run when they hear the words "marriage this year" on a first date.
6. Talk about your psychic or astrologer and how you always take to heart what they tell you. You can also mention that one of them told you how perfect the two of you are together. It makes you seem like you just walked off the "Twilight Zone" set. Chances are he'll feel pretty uncomfortable and will exit pretty quickly.
7. Start yawning over and over again while your date is talking. Then tell him you've had a long day, you're really tired and have to get up early the next day so you're going to cut the date short.

8. Don't laugh but spilling something on your clothing is a way to make a fast exit. You might want to order a glass of water with whatever else you're drinking since it won't stain.

9. You can always say you're not feeling well. With the flu as rampant as it is in certain seasons, most men will want to avoid you like the plague.

Can You Ask Him Out First?

"The Secret of Attraction is to love oneself." ~Deepak Chopra

As a woman, your main job in the dating world is to signal a single man when you're interested in him. It's his job to ask you out.

Men are really scared of being rejected by women so it's going to take some encouragement on your part to let him know he can safely approach you.

Let's review how to let him know you're approachable. Begin by smiling at a man as you pass by him. You'll want to hold eye contact for five seconds. If he's interested, he'll approach.

Get in the habit of asking men questions wherever you are. And it doesn't matter if he's a datable man or not. You just want to start interacting with male energy as often as you can.

Here's an approach that throws caution to the wind but if you want him to notice you, it's a sure-fire way to get his attention. Go up to a guy and say, "Hi, my name is Sara. I'd love if you'd come over and say hi to my friend and me."

Even better – a line that leaves no doubt you're interested is to go up to a man and say, "Hi, I'm Sara. If you're single and interested in getting to know me better, here's my number. I'd love to go out with you if you ask me." Wink at him, smile and then walk away.

Leading a guy is going to take you out of your comfort zone but sometimes that's what you may have to do to make your dreams of being with Mr. Right come true. Even though you see men in the movies coming on to women in bars or restaurants, in real life, this is a rarity.

Men are truly afraid to come near you. They are afraid you'll reject them so the bolder you are in getting his attention by flirting and being playful, the better.

How To Have A Great First Date

"If you can't say something nice about yourself, practice."

~Author Unknown

You can start by leaving your past in the past. As the saying goes, "What happens in Vegas, stays in Vegas." The same goes for your ex on a first date. Leave him out of the conversation other than to say you were married and divorced.

Beware of how much information you disclose at this point. You might think you're doing both of you a favor laying out the good, the bad and the ugly about you and your life on the table. In some ways, you're testing him to see if he can accept all of that about you. It's not fair to either of you to do this.

Think about how would you feel if a man told you all his problems on your first date. Chances are you'd run. It's way too emotionally overwhelming. And it's a turn off.

A first date is just a meet and greet to determine if you'd like to get to know each other better. The information a man can handle further in the dating cycle is totally different than what he wants or needs to know on a first date.

Remember, you are far more than your problems so he doesn't need to know them all at this point.

Always be sure conversation has a good give and take balance to it. When people are nervous they have a tendency to talk a lot about themselves to fill the silent gaps that can happen. This doesn't work well on a date. In fact, it's really boring for the one who has to listen to a running monologue.

Ask a man a lot of questions. If you find yourself talking continuously for more than a minute or two without him saying a word, you are probably over-talking.

A first date is a time for sharing a lot of surface information about your likes and interests on different topics. Your goal is to find the common threads between you to see if you want to take this to a second date.

I will tell you, men will gab on and on when they are

trying to impress you. Make it your job to find a place to jump in and share when you can relate to something he's saying.

Otherwise, you'll leave the date with him thinking you have nothing to say. And you'll leave thinking he's a rude man who never shuts up.

Work hard to be present while you're on a date with a new man.

Put your cell phone away so you can give your full attention to your date. He wants to feel as if you're interested in getting to know him and that he is more important than anything your phone might be showing you at the moment.

Plus, you may have noticed this already - as we age, multi-tasking is a lot harder to do. You'll probably find you didn't hear a word he said if you're on your phone, texting while he's talking. It's pretty embarrassing to look up over your reading glasses and say, "Could you please repeat that?"

If you like a man on a first date, you can gently touch his arm or his hand when making a point or when flirting. A man sees this type of physical contact as a sign of encouragement and it shows him that you're interested.

Unless you want to date a Beta Male and be the Alpha yourself, be as feminine as you can and allow the man to have control over the date.

We, as women, are so used to taking care of others and anticipating their needs that we forget and automatically start trying to make life easier for the man sitting across the table from us. He's a big boy and can fend for himself. Stop yourself from doing this before it starts!

Let him take care of the bad service or the bad food. Don't tell him how he should have handled a situation and for sure, don't criticize him for what he eats or how he walks or talks.

If you find you don't like the way a man handles his life, then walk away. There is someone else out there better suited for you.

Who Should Pay The Bill?

"Your boyfriend should not be your source of income, my dear. It's a relationship, not a job opportunity."
~Author Unknown

I'm often asked whether a woman should offer to split the check with a man on a first date. My answer is – not unless you were the one to ask him out. Allow a man to pay for the first 3 dates, including the initial meet and greet.

After that, you can offer to pick up the check or make him dinner. Now if he tells you he's on a tight budget, then offer sooner. But if you're with a successful Alpha Male, don't even think about splitting a first date check. He'll be insulted. It's his pleasure to take care of you this way.

If you're only interested in creating a friendship with a man, splitting the check is fine. But if it's a romance you want, allow him to pay at least through the third date.

At that point, you can offer to pay for popcorn at the movies. Or make him dinner. Single men love a good home-cooked meal. Once you're in the relationship, the two of you can work out how to deal with the money issue based on both your financial situations.

He Walks You To Your Car... Now What?

"If you don't know your own worth and value, then do not expect someone else to calculate it for you." ~Author Unknown

Elizabeth met a nice man for lunch and had a lovely time. She always gave her dates a quick kiss on the lips along with a hug as they said goodbye. She assumed this is how it would be with this gentleman as well.

As he walked her to the car, he opened the door, she put her purse in the car and turned to do her customary end of date ritual…a quick kiss on the lips and a hug.

She was taken aback when he bypassed the quick kiss and proceeded to ram his tongue into her mouth. Totally embarrassed by his behavior in such a public place, Elizabeth was perplexed why he'd do this.

A man who does this is extremely attracted to you. Does he overstep a boundary giving you this type of kiss in such a public place? Yes, but most men will try and get away with whatever they can with you. They will push to see what your limit is.

The way to handle this is to decide, before you even start

dating, what you are willing to do on a first date when it comes to kissing and sex, especially if you find yourself really attracted to a man.

If you're attracted, chances are, a slow, lingering kiss will feel great to you. But if it doesn't feel good to you on a first date, yet you like the guy and would be open to a second date, all you have to do is gently say, "I so appreciate you wanting to kiss me but this feels uncomfortable for me right now. Would it be okay if we save this type of kissing for a time when we know each other better?"

You're not demanding what you want. You are getting him to step up to be your hero by using this softer type of language.

By using language from your truest feminine side, a man won't feel judged or embarrassed for showing you how much he's attracted to you.

How To Get A Second Date

"Some people come into our lives and quickly go. Some people move our souls to dance. Some people make the sky more beautiful to gaze upon. They stay in our lives for a while, leave footprints on our hearts, and we are never, ever the same again."
~Author Unknown

THE WINNING DATING FORMULA FOR WOMEN OVER 50

Of course a lot goes into whether or not a second date ever happens, but I'd say the woman who consistently gets asked out again does so because she makes a man feel good about being a man. In her eyes, he's awesome exactly how he is.

Men would often tell me I was the best date they'd ever been on. The reason was, I let him be a man and my hero while we were together.

It's important to come from that softer side of you that we talked about earlier in this book. He'll love when you talk from your heart, not your head.

I don't mean saying "I love you" or even "I like you." What I mean is using sentences that start with words like "I feel" rather than the more masculine "I think."

When you ask a man a lot of questions, it shows you're interested in him, plus it gives him the simple of gift of boosting his ego. Everyone can use more of this type of encouragement.

Let him open the door for you. If you drop something, let him pick it up for you. These make a man feel his most masculine. He is extremely attracted to the woman who can bring this out in him.

A man once told me he was on a date with a woman he thought might be perfect for him based on an online profile. They were walking along a trail and it was hilly. He was in front of her. He turned around and noticed that she appeared to be having difficulty maneuvering the trail.

He reached back and extended his hand to help her. In what he heard as a domineering tone, she told him she could do it on her own.

As a man, he felt shot done for doing what a man's suppose to do, be a woman's hero. Needless to say, he didn't ask her out again.

Silly things beyond our control can stall the dating process from going any further past the initial meet and greet. It can be something goofy like you have the same purse as his ex. Or you spoke to the waiter in the same tone his last girlfriend used that drove him crazy so it sent him running.

You probably do the same thing. Just think about the great guy you met who was perfect, until he opened his mouth and showed you his not-so-perfect yellow teeth.

Another reason a second date doesn't happen is because you don't match the picture in his head of who he thinks he wants to spend the rest of his life with.

A man scans your profile and contacts you if he thinks you fit this picture. The two of you are on the phone talking the hours away, and his fantasy picture is working overtime, thinking you might be the one. You get excited thinking maybe he's right for you, too!

Then the two of you meet and within minutes, he's

decided you aren't a match to what he thought he wanted so the second date doesn't happen.

Making a man feel great about who he is by allowing him to be your hero may give him pause and cause him to create a new fantasy picture that could be you.

One of the greatest gifts you can give yourself is to not take dating too personally. If you do, dating will become a dreaded chore versus the fun journey it can be of meeting someone new and interesting who might make a good friend, lover or even boyfriend once you get to know each other.

When a second date doesn't happen, instead of feeling sad, get yourself back online. Or head out into the real world to meet men who will be a better fit for you.

Why First Date Booty Calls Rarely Turn Into A Second Date

You meet a man... the chemistry is hot and as the date ends, the two of you start kissing and kissing and kissing some more. Hands start roving all over the place and you find yourself in the back seat of his car having sex with a man you've only known for a few hours.

You're both on fire... it feels good and it feels right... he tells you your great but days go by and he doesn't call. Why? It was too easy for him.

Men categorize the women they date into two groups. The first are the women they play with. It's easy sex. It's fun for him but that's all it is.

There's no emotional attachment or connection to you on his part and that's why few first dates make it to second ones when sex has been involved from the get go.

Then there is Category number two. This is when he thinks of you as a Potential Relationship Match and he's likely to ask you out again.

When you really want a man in your life, your energy can give off the scent of neediness. For most men this is a pretty scary thought to have to deal with a needy woman.

Here's a great example of how this happens. You're having an amazing first date. Your mind is working overtime, as you imagine the life the two of you can have together. Things are going so well, you start telling him how nice it would be to move in with him.

Nothing scares a man or turns him off faster than a woman who is already making her life his life. This is the time to slow things down and get to know someone before deciding he is the one you'd like to share a commitment with.

Remember that first date behavior is nothing more than good behavior. It's not real life behavior. It takes a while to really get to know someone. So, let yourself enjoy the process of this special time before the real work of a relationship begins.

This is the sweetest time in most new relationships when everything is a fairy tale.

In the meantime, keep your own apartment. Create a life you love so you have cool and interesting things of your own to share with him when you get together.

As you can see there are lots of reasons men don't call you back for a second date. I've only listed a few here. Save yourself a lot of date analysis and evaluation by not being invested in its outcome. If it's meant to be, it will be.

Five Guys Not Worth A Second Date

"I'd like to say thank you to all the people who came into my life and made it outstanding and also to all the people who walked out of my life and made it fantastic!" ~Someecards

The first is the man who disappears and comes back with no good explanation. Your dates with this man have been fun and he has most of the qualities on your Wish List.

When you're together, you laugh a lot. Conversation between the two of you is easy and you're beginning to like this guy, thinking he just might be the one.

Then out of nowhere, he disappears, showing up again six months later, texting you that he's missed both you and your kisses but can't seem to explain why he went AWOL.

If he was into you, he'd have texted you during his hiatus. After all, there is a popular gadget called a smart phone that can text and dial quite well from anywhere in the world.

A man would never tolerate this type of behavior from a woman. Neither should you from a man unless he tells you what happened in those six months… Plus exactly why he went AWOL and why he's now back.

This guy has a secret life he isn't sharing. You don't need men like this in your life who are here today and gone tomorrow with no explanations.

Don't give him a second chance. He's not worth it unless he went off to war or works in the government and goes on secret missions. In that case, he's probably making that up so dump him.

Guy number two is the type who texts at his convenience when he wants to go out. This man is thoughtless. Texting you to go on a date versus calling is a sign of laziness.

Texting is impersonal and keeps you at arms length. A man who's into you wants to hear your voice and connect with you on a regular basis. Text this one back that you're not interested! His inability to connect on a more personal level makes him a waste of your time.

Our third guy is always working or spending time with his grandchildren. Work is the mistress for men who have a "type A" personality. They thrive on the excitement it brings to their lives.

And if you have grandchildren, you know what a blessing they can be but there is a life beyond them. If a man wants a relationship with you, he'll do what it takes to create the space and the balance in his life so he can see you. If he doesn't, his actions are showing you he's not into you. This man is not worth a second date ever! He's not going to change.

The fourth guy who doesn't deserve a second chance is the one who introduces you to everyone as his friend. When a man's into you, he wants the world to know it.

He's proud to have you on his arm and he'll excitedly introduce you as this great girl he's just met, or if you've been dating a while, as his girlfriend. If he introduces you as a friend, that's what you are and it's not likely to change.

Men mean what they say. Don't expect anymore from this guy other than friendship. Sorry to say, he's just not seeing you as girlfriend material.

He's a great guy to hang out with but don't let him take you away from meeting the guy who wants you as his girlfriend.

Last but not least, our fifth guy who's not worth the time of day when it comes to second dates is the one who wants the date to happen at your place or his place. He's not into going out.

This guy is looking for a booty call. The man is physically attracted to you and can literally charm the pants off of you. He'll say words that lead you to believe he's into you. He likes you but his mission is to get you into bed and that's why he'll always suggest intimate dinners at one of your places.

Whenever he's feeling the sexual urge, he comes back for more. Here's the problem with this guy. As a woman, you bond having sex. Men don't and this means a guy like this can really hurt you when he's not into you the same way you're into him. Let him go sooner rather than later. You deserve a guy who wants a real relationship!

"Find someone who isn't afraid to admit that they miss you. Someone who knows you're not perfect but treats you as if

you are. Someone whose biggest fear is losing you. One who gives their heart completely. Someone who says I love you and means it. Last but not least, find someone you wouldn't mind waking up with you in the morning, seeing your wrinkles and your gray hair but still falls in love with you all over again."

~Author Unknown

Should You Call Him After A Date?

"First Date Rules...Real men call!"

-Author Unknown

Annie met a great guy through a mutual friend at a party. They laughed and talked for about an hour and then exchanged phone numbers. A couple of days passed and she hadn't heard from him. She decided to give him a call, hoping it would remind him of the fun they'd shared together at the party.

After talking for an hour, she suggested since they were having so much fun they should meet for drinks. They did and again shared a lot of laughter and good conversation. He said he'd call, but a week went by without hearing from him. She really wanted to call him again. I'll tell you what Annie asked me. Should she call him?

The answer is NO!
You do not call a man this early in the game.

A man's actions speak louder than his words. If a man takes your number but doesn't call you, it means he's not interested in pursuing a relationship with you right now.

What's so crazy is he can have the best time talking with you over and over again, and as you already know, if you don't fit that picture in his head of who his woman needs to be, he's not going to pursue you.

Then why does he take your number if he's not really interested? A man doesn't want to hurt your feelings. So to appear nice, he'll take it if you offer it. Yet chances are if he didn't ask you for it in the first place, it's likely he'll put it in his shirt pocket and forget it's even there.

He's trying not to hurt you and that's the reason he'll ignore your texts, emails or Facebook postings. In his mind, he's justifying his actions, thinking, *if I don't answer her I won't hurt her.*

As hard as it feels, you have to let a man lead when it comes to contacting you.

Chemistry... What It Is And Isn't

"No, this trick won't work...

How on earth are you ever going to explain in terms of chemistry and physics so important a biological phenomenon as first love?"
~Albert Einstein

Jenna had dated quite a few men after her divorce but not one had come close to being as physically attractive to her as her ex was. Even though they'd divorced years ago, the sexual chemistry they'd shared still lingered within her.

She was finding it extremely difficult to not compare her ex to these new men. It left her wondering if she'd ever find chemistry like this again. She knew the men she was dating would make far better partners but she yearned for that chemistry she'd once shared with this man in her past.

The type of chemistry Jenna was looking for is actually an exciting chemical cocktail your body produces to create an intense rush when you meet someone you're attracted to.

It's called oxytocin and it's highly addictive, it feels good and it lasts about 90 days before you see a man for who he really is. This type of chemistry cannot be sustained and when the flaws of a man begin showing up, you start questioning what made you get involved with him in the first place.

If you meet a man and feel this type of chemistry, do yourself a favor and run the other way as fast as you can. That is unless you are looking for a lot of sex and nothing else with a man. It's almost impossible to turn what's happening here into a true relationship.

The best chemistry is one that develops over time and might not start appearing until date three or four. This type of chemistry is sustainable and makes for a great relationship.

Now, if hot and sexy is all you want, by all means go for the oxytocin rush. Just know that it's a chemical reaction that will probably end within three months.

If you have a first date with a man and you feel like the instant chemistry is missing, try going out with him again to see if it develops over time. I had a client who went out with a nice man three times and kept wondering why she was hanging in there when she felt nothing.

On the fourth date, he reached across the table, touched her face and the chemistry sparked for her. They ended up in a great relationship together.

If you are looking for *big bang chemistry* – the kind that makes you feel this huge immediate connection with a man – it is more than likely a chemical reaction happening between your bodies that usually doesn't turn out well for either of you.

Just remember the good kind of chemistry can take some time to build. If after four dates you still aren't feeling anything, then it probably is time to move on.

Dating And Sex After 50

"For the first time in history, sex is more dangerous than the cigarette afterward." ~Jay Leno

Sex over 50. Some women can't wait to have it again and some women feel that's all men seem to want. Most are confused as to what the rules about sex are at our age. Let's clear this issue up once and for all.

Before we go any further, it's important to note that sexually transmitted diseases or STDs, in our age group are on the rise, so practicing safe sex is a must for every woman over 50 these days. Now that worries over pregnancy are no longer an issue, we think we can be lax in this department. Don't be.

Always carry some type of protection with you so that when hormones heat up, you are protected. Sounds a lot like our teen years, doesn't it? A great source for more information on this topic is your doctor. With this out of the way, lets get to some common questions about sex and dating.

Let's start with when is it okay to have sex? As we've talked about, sometimes we have such strong chemistry with a man that we hop into bed with him on date number one.

Hey, our hormonal urges sometimes need a good fix and there is nothing wrong with that.

First date sex is usually just that – a fix that doesn't go much further. It's a fun fling and the best way to avoid it is to keep a first date under two hours. This way you won't risk feeling so connected that you want to have sex with a man right away. More on that to come...

You'll often hear that date number three is the sex date. This is urban legend for women our age. Of course, you can have sex on the third date if you'd like. Just be sure to go with your instincts and whether or not it feels right for you.

Take your time. Don't allow men to pressure you into moving too quickly into a physical relationship until you know what it is you want to do. If he's not willing to honor your wishes, he is not the right man for you.

That being said, men need encouragement that they are not sitting in the friend zone with you. This means some good kissing and maybe even a little touchy feely action by the third date. Otherwise, men put you in the friend zone and disappear.

There are still men out there who want fast and easy sex. Be sure your online profile doesn't mention anything about sex, making love or how long it's been since you've had sex.

This sends the wrong message to men and when it's there in black and white for a man to read on his computer, he will assume that it is sex – not a relationship – you are looking for.

My best advice about sex is to always follow your instincts. Although if the sexual pull is super strong right away, remember this is *hot chemistry*. Be careful and go slow if this is the case.

You want a relationship built on a foundation of friendship because once the sex wanes, if friendship isn't there, the relationship with nothing left to support it will crumble.

"There are three possible parts to a date, of which at least two must be offered: entertainment, food, and affection. It is customary to begin a series of dates with a great deal of entertainment, a moderate amount of food, and the merest suggestion of affection. As the amount of affection increases, the entertainment can be reduced proportionately. When the affection is the entertainment, we no longer call it dating. Under no circumstances can the food be omitted."
~Miss Manners' Guide to Excruciatingly Correct Behavior

He Asks What You're Wearing

You're online and a man contacts you who initially sounds really nice. Before long, he starts talking about sex in a joking kind of way or he starts asking you what you're wearing. Why do men do this and what should you do?

This is an awkward situation that women often encounter during their dating journey. A man doing this is not looking for a relationship. He's basically on the prowl looking for a woman who will agree to have sex with him.

This is a man who is all about fulfilling his own needs and not yours.

If you are having one of those hormonal moments where you are looking for a sexual partner, you always have the option to meet him and see where it goes. But be sure you are SAFE about it. Use protection and always, always, always let someone know where you are and who you are with.

If it's a relationship you want, don't waste another moment interacting with this type of man. End your contact with him than go back to the dating site and block him from being able to reach you again!

There are plenty of great men out there looking for what you want and your time will be better spent getting to know someone who respects you and is looking for the same type of relationship you want.

Sexting

A woman has sex out of love for a man. Yet a man has sex to see if he can find love with a woman. This can lead to some mighty interesting text messages sent your way by men on the hunt for love.

What these men end up doing is "sexting" you. Chances are, your single kids are doing this. It's like the mating call of the 21st century.

What men don't understand is that most women our age get turned off by sexting, especially when it's with a man she hasn't even met. It goes back to the days when we were supposed to be the good girls, not the sex-crazed bad ones.

What you want to understand is that men are very visual and his first attraction to you will be based on sex and whether or not he wants to sleep with you. Sex is first in a man's mind, possibly leading him to fall in love with you.

We as women want to fall in love first, or at least in "like," with a man before we even think about sex. This is a classic example of a "men are from Mars, women are from Venus" situation with each of us speaking a different language when it comes to love and sex.

It is a compliment but one that can often feel yucky to a woman.

We want to be respected by men and this direction feels disrespectful to us, especially when it happens right away with him pawing us in person or "sexting" us before we've met.

It's ok to say, "I feel uncomfortable with this."

If he doesn't stop, let him know you aren't interested and move on to someone who understands more about what you as a woman really wants and needs.

What To Do If He Sends You A Picture of His Privates

When a man is excited to be with you, he might try and impress you by sending pictures of his "stuff." And I'm not talking about the junk lying around the house. You see-exchanging pictures of each other's private parts is a turn on for some men, and he thinks it is for you too.

What he doesn't realize is this photographic exchange is not necessarily doing anything for you other than freaking you out. If you decide you want to play in the sandbox with him and send pictures back, it's okay as long as you're comfortable with it.

But do be wary of sending images of your private parts via today's technology. If you do, you just might find yourself on the Internet as the next over 50's pinup girl when a relationship sours.

Picture exchanging is more likely to happen when you get involved with younger men. They are just so proud of their penises, they feel obligated to share the joy with you.

First Date Sex

If you have sex on the first date with a man, you're not alone. Lots of women have done the same thing. And it's so easy to beat yourself up when something like this takes place. I hope you will forgive yourself once you understand what really happened on your date.

Let's face it, sometimes your hormones can just take over and that's why it's important to make **sexual and personal safety** a priority when you are dating. When this situation happens, it's because you've probably spent too much time on a first date sharing details about your lives with each other.

This creates a false sense of closeness that can lead to lots of kissing and touching.

Then with your hormones raging, you begin to feel emotionally close to a man after sharing so much with each other. So you end up making the choice to have sex with him. And what occurs? You bond with him.

What gets a woman into trouble is believing he bonds with you too. All a man has to do is feel sexually attracted to have sex with you. That's it!

He doesn't bond and that's why he can have a one night stand and walk away so easily. To him it was just pleasurable sex. You have two choices here. You can continue beating yourself up or you can view the whole thing as a learning experience.

The best gift you can give yourself is to decide what your sexual boundaries are before you start dating. Start by deciding what you're willing to do and when you're willing to do it. Even write this down in a journal so you have something to refer back to when your hormones are raging.

Sexual Dysfunction After 50

Lots of men these days are vying for the attention of a woman over 50, as I've noted before. Now more than ever you have a choice of who to date and have a sexual relationship with... whether it's with younger men, older men or men your own age.

There are advantages to each. Younger men have the sexual stamina you may be looking for and seem to have more balanced masculine and feminine sides to them. Hanging out in bed all day might feel pretty good but when the sex is done, you may realize you have very little in common to talk about.

Men closer to your age share a history with you that is nice. He'll remember the Beatles appearance on Ed Sullivan or the Apollo landing on the moon. But like his older counterpart, sexual dysfunction can start showing up once he hits his 50's.

Men over 50, even with products like Viagra and Cialis, may no longer be able to hold a solid continuous erection. Many of the medicines men take to relieve health issues like diabetes, heart problems and blood pressure can cause this as well. And, testosterone levels have diminished as men have aged, creating erection issues.

This can be challenging, especially if intercourse is considered the only form of acceptable lovemaking for you. Be kind to these men. This is very hard on them as it truly takes away their feelings of masculinity.

If you're willing to be flexible, these men can make good lovers, doing everything to please you as they compensate for what they are no longer able to do.

Are You Addicted To Love?

"Love is a matter of chemistry, but sex is a matter of physics."
~Author Unknown

I had a client I'll call Sandy, who loved a man named Jeff with all her heart. Yet they had broken up at least three times during the two and a half years they'd been together.

While apart, an intense longing for the other would occur. They'd come back together celebrating a harmonious honeymoon truce with a lot of love and a lot of sex. But it wouldn't take long for the problems creating the break up to reappear.

Sandy didn't understand why love wasn't enough to work through the difficulties that always seemed to show up. She and Jeff were so different. Her friends couldn't understand why she was even with him. To them, she and Jeff didn't see life in the same way.

She was a Ritz kind of girl and he was a camping dude. She could get past all of this because she felt their heart connection would sustain them through thick and thin. It had up until then.

But she had tired of his habit of taking off on his little trips to explore the countryside without her. And she found trying to get a commitment from him just to go to dinner with friends was like pulling teeth.

She wanted more from him. She really wanted their relationship to go to the next level. He was a good man and even though they didn't have a lot in common, she could feel him in her heart all the time.

She even knew when he was thinking about her, making it feel like he was always with her even when he wasn't. And that brought her tremendous comfort.

So was Sandy really in love or was she addicted to Jeff? More than likely, it was the chemical addiction to Oxytocin that occurs when a woman bonds with a man.

What did I advise Sandy to do? And what can you do about it if you find yourself addicted to love?

You'll want to understand that Oxytocin creates a high in a woman that is often mistaken for love. The longing for the other person is actually a craving for the high when the chemical is released into the body. Just thinking about the other person or hearing their voice can release the drug.

The great sex after a breakup was like a fix. Oxytocin was released and the high happened producing a sense of comfort just like heroin would to an addict.

If you believe you may have an Oxytocin addiction to a man, one of the ways to tell is to ask yourself what you really love about a man.

It's important to hone in on the qualities he brings to the table beyond sex and love that make you feel good being in a relationship with him.

Next, ask yourself what you don't love or like about him. Sandy and Jeff continued breaking up for a reason. He wasn't committed, she needed more from him and he wasn't able to give it.

Next check in and determine whether or not what he brings to the table is enough for you and the relationship you desire with him.

When it's an Oxytocin addiction, there's usually not enough beyond sex, love and a heart connection. Almost everything else is annoying, irritating and feels unsolvable.

To release the addiction, get yourself busy. Date other men. Go out with friends or family. Volunteer. Take a class because the longing will come back and you need to be prepared when it does.

An Oxytocin addiction can stay with you for years. To break it, start by acknowledging this chemical addiction is what your relationship is about.

Stop all contact with this man, whether it's talking on the phone, emailing him, texting him, checking him out on Facebook or seeing him in person. Otherwise the addiction will start all over again.

You can do it. As with any addiction, it takes time to recover. Be kind to yourself, especially when you're frustrated, feeling like it will never go away.

Do things that feel good. Often having contact with him after the initial high goes away doesn't. Get some friends together to be your support group. You will feel like a freak at times but know you aren't alone. Or get professional help if it continues for longer than nine months to a year.

This happens to normal people. The key is identifying the addiction so you can take the steps to overcome the Oxytocin high and move on.

Friends With Benefits

"I'd like to meet the man who invented sex and see what he's working on now." ~*Author Unknown*

Diane and Alan had been seeing each other for about a year in a *friends with benefits* relationship. At around the eighth month mark, Diane's emotions started changing and she began falling for him.

Alan texted her constantly and he spent every chance he got at Diane's home hanging out with her. The two spent a lot of time watching their favorite TV shows or talking the night away sharing their lives with each other.

When she was sick, she felt so grateful when he tended to her every need until she felt better. And the sex between the two of them was off-the-charts fantastic!

Then one day Alan just stopped coming around and Diane had no idea what had happened. She'd tried texting him but got no replies.

Then she got a message from her girlfriend telling her that Alan was spending his time with her and would be proclaiming his love for her on Facebook in the next day or two.

Diane was so confused and hurt by Alan's actions. She couldn't understand how he could go from hot to cold literally overnight. Unfortunately, what happened to Diane is pretty common in friends with benefits relationships.

Again, your heart bonds with a man when you have a physical relationship with him. Yet a man's heart does not need to be connected when he is in a physical relationship with you. That's why a man is able to walk away so easily when he's done.

It's a fun casual relationship for him with a LOT OF BENEFITS while he's in it! And his signals can be so confusing, causing you to think you've moved into a heart-centered, real relationship like when Alan cared for Diane when she was sick.

Men love the friendship connection they can have with women and remember this man was Diane's friend. That is part of why he took care of her when she was sick.

The chemistry was great for both of them, causing the physical relationship to feel so off-the-charts wonderful. But when one person starts falling for the other in this type of relationship, a conversation needs to happen to see if both of you are still on the same relationship page.

Unless a man expresses the desire to be in a long-term relationship with you, he isn't feeling like you're "the one" for him. He will leave when he's had enough or found someone else, leaving your heart in crumbled pieces.

He drops out of sight because men don't like to hurt women. In his mind, ignoring you meant he wasn't hurting you. Of course, it does hurt but he doesn't see it this way.

Due to the heart bonding you can feel with a man once you become intimate, women are usually the big losers in friend with benefits relationships when the men they fall for move on.

Who Should Be The First To Say I Love You?

"Every girl's dream is to have a guy call her at 3 AM just to say, 'Hey baby, I just want to tell you I love you am outside of your window with chocolate chip cookies and ice cream.'"

~Author Unknown

Well ladies, it's the man who should always be the first to say those 3 words you want to hear. Why? He needs to be the one to show you he's interested in being in a committed relationship with you. Then it's up to you to decide if you want this as well.

This is part of why men think women have all the power in the dating arena. A man is afraid of rejection. So if a man ever says, "I love you," and you don't love him back, be kind. He made himself totally vulnerable by expressing his feelings for you.

If you say it first, he might run if he's not ready. So as hard as it is, work at keeping this strong feeling to yourself. If too much time goes by and he hasn't expressed the "L word," it might be a sign he's not seeing you as a long-term partner. If that's your goal, you might want to move on to find a man who wants to be on the same page as you.

Dating and Gifts

"If you wait to do everything until you're sure it's right you'll probably never do much of anything." ~Life: live it

Elayna had been dating Jerrod for a month. His birthday was coming up and she wasn't sure what she should do. She knew he'd love having an iPod mini so he had something to listen to when he walked the track at his gym. Even though they'd been intimate, she wasn't sure whether it was an appropriate gift so early for a dating relationship.

When you've only been dating a month, even if you have been intimate, it's smart to keep the gift on the less expensive side. A nice gift would be a home cooked meal of his favorite foods.

Or if he's a coffee junkie, gift certificates to his favorite coffee shop are a great gift. If he turns his Keurig on before he leaves the house, find out his favorite flavor and buy a box for his special day. A favorite bottle of wine is another good gift.

These are appropriate gifts when you've become exclusive but still don't know each other that well. Think about saving extravagant gifts for later on if the relationship continues to grow into a long-term commitment.

What To Do When Friends Don't Like A New Boyfriend

"If what you see by the eye doesn't please you, then close your eyes and see from the heart. Because the heart can see beauty and love more than the eyes can ever wonder." ~Author Unknown

Colleen met a really nice man named Jim online. He was a terrible dresser and at times she was embarrassed to be seen in public with him. They had different lifestyles, which concerned her. They both loved to travel but she was a classy kind of gal and his tastes were more like a 60's hippy travelling down the road camping in his VW van.

What pulled her into the relationship was the way Jim worshipped and adored her. He'd do anything for her; something she'd never experienced before. Colleen found herself developing feelings for this man.

He was really funny, he was super smart, kind and she enjoyed being with him. Yet her friends thought she was nuts, telling her he was way beneath her.

Friends are not always thrilled with your choices when it comes to the men you date. They mean well, giving their opinions, thinking they are being helpful to you. Yet what they usually do is judge a man based on who he appears to be on the outside. In this case, looking only at his clothes and lifestyle choices. These are changeable qualities if a man wants to change them.

Sometimes only you are able to see the wonderful internal qualities and values a man has.

In Colleen's situation her man showed kindness, intelligence and an ability to make her laugh. These are great qualities that friends might not see until they spend time getting to know someone.

Men are pretty simple creatures. So when it comes to travel, luxury may not be a priority to Jim as it is for Colleen. It's also possible a man you date may not have the money needed for the lifestyle you desire.

Regardless of who friends think you should be with, the question to ask yourself is: are you ok with this lifestyle difference? If you really like a man who can give to you in other ways, would you be willing to compromise on your differences?

In Colleen's case, would she foot the whole bill for the hotel she desires or let him pay towards her kind of hotel, the same amount he'd have paid for a Super 8?

These are qualities that can be figured out with good communication skills; meaning they are workable.

Friends aren't on the inside of your relationship to see how the two of you are in private.

The only time friends have the right to judge is when they are aware of internal qualities that are not fixable or changeable in a man. Qualities like meanness that you might excuse or even miss while you are falling for who you think he is.

If he's a man who wants to please you and do for you, he's a good man worth getting to know. Unless you live with your friends, try not letting them influence your decision to date a man based on his clothes or his car. Overtime, hopefully, your friends will come around when they see you are happy.

They say people come in our lives for a season, a time or a reason and that we learn about ourselves from every relationship, so just enjoy a man while you are with him.

And remember, you don't have to marry him. As a woman over 50, you can just appreciate his companionship and have fun while you're together!

Getting Out Of A Dating Rut

"Nothing every goes away until it teaches us what we need to know." ~Pema Chodra

Now I want to talk to you about three ways to get yourself out of a dating rut and into the magical dating life you desire. Often women come to work with me when they have hit a wall in their dating lives. Things aren't going well, they aren't meeting the guys they want to meet and even worse, no one is noticing them online or in the real world.

I want you to know that this happens to every woman at every level of dating. Believe me, I see it over and over again. I experienced it! And when it happens, it doesn't feel good.

What ends up happening is you start blaming yourself because nothing you're doing seems to be working.

I've got three ways to help you get out of your dating rut and get you back out there having fun dating while finding a great guy at this time in your life.

Step one is to realize that you're not alone. When things don't go the way you think they should, you tend to think, "Well, everybody else is out there dating good guys. They're doing great." And you feel like no one else is frustrated and struggling with dating. It feels like you're the only one!

Well, that's simply not true. Why? Most women put their best self out there for the world to see. Think about how many times you didn't let anyone know when things weren't going well. I see it all the time – women around the country and around the world – it happens to everyone.

Understand that even though it looks like everybody else is out there dating amazing men and you feel like the only one out who isn't.... it's not the case. Understand that and have some compassion for yourself.

Step two – It's time to build your confidence back up. When it feels like nothing is happening in your dating life, it sometimes makes you feel depressed or has you doubt your attractiveness to men. The number one thing that needs to happen is building your dating confidence back up. In fact, this one thing touches every single aspect of your life.

Confidence touches how you will get out there and talk to the men you want to date. Confidence affects how you appear to men. Confidence affects the men you want to be attracting. It affects everything about your dating life so it's important that you really keep your confidence really high.

I don't mean acting superior, conceited or egotistical — it's an inner knowing that you're an amazing woman just as you are!

You've got to protect your confidence. The way to do this sounds kind of funny, but it works. I suggest creating a list of the amazing qualities you possess... 10-15 about your physical self, 10-15 about your personality and 10-15 about what you're good at and interested in.

Then every morning or every time you pass a mirror remind yourself of two or three of the qualities you love about you. You'll find that you start liking the woman you see in the mirror every day. And when you're having a bad day, you can give yourself a little boost of confidence using these lists.

I did this a lot, especially after a date went south. It was key in keeping my confidence up so I could get back out there and date when I didn't feel like it.

Step three is that we have to get you off the dime by taking action! If you stay at home thinking *woe is me*, or you sit around with friends complaining there are no good men out there to date... well, there comes a point where it has to end.   You realize now that you're not the only one, that it's temporary. You've built up your confidence, so now it's time to get going and take massive action that's going to get you out there dating the guys you want.

Think about this... What did you used to do that got you dates with good guys, that you have somehow stopped doing? Did you used to try different online dating sites and you stopped? Did you talk to men in the real world, but then you stopped? Did you take classes about dating or even get group or one on one coaching then stopped using what you learned?

Listen, we're putting it all out here on the table. Did you get lazy? Did you start resting on your laurels? Notice what you used to do that you're no longer doing and then do that again.

Now I'd like you to think about what you are resisting. What have you been resisting? Have you resisted trying out that new dating site? Write the things down that you are resisting and then take action on those.

Your Assignment for Creating a Magical Dating Life After 50.

You can have all these great ideas but you do not get results from things you do not implement. This is what I tell my clients all the time. The difference between a successful person and a person who struggles is that the successful person will do what others aren't willing to do. This is part of the mindset to get you out of your rut, past your obstacles and into the magical dating life you desire.

Take the three steps we just went through and put them to work. I used this process whenever I hit a stumbling block in my dating life. It works!

Once you understand that you're not the only one who gets in a dating rut, then build your confidence back up and start taking action to change your dating life, you'll see everything start to happen for you.

Handling Your Dating Frustrations

"Here's to all of you who rearrange the dirty dishes in the dishwasher after someone else has loaded it." ~Someecards

Have there been times in your life when you've gotten frustrated with dating and found yourself tired of trying to find Mr. Right?

Those are the moments when you feel like there is just no one out there to date anymore – every good guy has been taken. You think at this point you'd just settle if someone halfway decent showed up in your life.

Many women get this way when they are being really picky about who they will date. They usually spend the first date looking for their idea of the *perfect man*, one who has certain characteristics like lots of money and/or good looks.

At the same time, they often pass up men who aren't the most handsome or wealthiest and yet they have a lot of great qualities like kindness or a willingness to do anything to make you happy.

Quality Men come in different packages so think about keeping your eyes and mind open to dating different types of men.

Often when we are frustrated with dating, we find ourselves feeling so lonely. We'd like to date but it feels like too much work for what we get back in return.

Dating is like finding a job. It requires a lot of patience and time each day to work the dating system. This means you want to spend 20-30 minutes a day at online dating sites looking for men you might be interested in. Or you can get yourself out into the world and find activities and places where you can interact with the types of men you'd like to date.

Just keep at it. You wouldn't quit looking for work if you needed a job. You'd keep going until you found one. The same goes for dating. As hard as it feels at times, don't stop looking for a Quality Man until you've found one to bring into your life.

You may have to kiss a few frogs along the way but the one you're looking for is out there waiting for you. You just have to keep working the dating system until you find him.

Texting... The New Way to Break Up

"Never get jealous when you see your ex with some else, because our parents taught us to give our used toys to the less fortunate."

~Author Unknown

Texting has become the new Dear John/Dear Jane way of ending relationships in the 21st century. I know this for a fact because it happened to me. I met a man at an internet dating site. He and I really hit it off. And let me tell you, he was some serious eye candy!

He was the first guy I ever dated where my knees nearly buckled when I saw him. Our relationship was easy and fun. We could talk for hours and somehow he was one of those guys that knew when something was wrong just from hearing my voice. A rarity!

Our problem was I travelled a lot during our short time together. We kept in touch over the phone and in our last conversation, he told me how much he missed me and how he couldn't wait until the next time we'd be together. So imagine my surprise when I arrived home and received this text:

"Hi Lisa, I've enjoyed our time together but I feel we got too close too fast. I really like you but I need some space. I'll call you in a few weeks."

I was stunned and I was pissed. I had no clue why he was blowing me off. Only days earlier, he had professed such care and concern for my well-being. But blow me off he did and in the most impersonal way possible. I texted him back hoping he would tell me why he was ending our relationship.

Of course, he didn't answer and that is why texting has become the new vehicle for relationship breakups. It's easy. There's no drama for the person creating the split. No having to answer the question, why. No seeing or hearing how the breakup may have hurt someone's feelings. Just a quick good bye and the relationship is done.

So why do I tell you this story? Because it could happen to you one day and I want you to be prepared if it does. You may feel bad and you may wonder why he broke up with you.

"So let's ignore each other, try to pretend the other person doesn't exist, but deep down, we both know it wasn't supposed to end like this." ~Author Unknown

Plus, the day may come where you try and do the same thing to a man you are dating. You might figure that if it was okay for someone to do it to you, then it's okay for you to do it to someone else.

Sadly, this technological way of breaking up will continue with quick, heart-breaking endings. With no closure for the victim of the break up text, it leaves them frustrated, trying to figure out what went wrong on their own.

My suggestion should this happen to you is to not text back. When he doesn't answer it will only frustrate you more.

Surviving A Break Up

"I had a lot of reasons to give up on you. But I still chose to stay. You had a lot of reasons to stay. But you chose to give up."

~Author Unknown

Breakups are hard on both the mind and the heart. The time after the breakup is a time of healing even when you were the one who initiated it. You'll want to do some processing and reflecting about the relationship before you head out to date again.

This is the perfect time for some personal reflection. Allow yourself to be open to answer questions like the ones I've listed below. They'll help you gain an understanding of what happened so you don't set yourself up to repeat similar dating and relationship patterns with a new man.

- **What did I love about this man?**
- **What didn't I love?**
- **What do I wish could have been different?**
- **What was my role in the relationship that contributed to the breakup?**
- **What are the lessons I learned from being with this man?**
- **What qualities from this man and this relationship would I like to take into my next one?**

As your healing and reflecting, be really kind to yourself. Treat yourself to a beautiful new journal and start *writing* all of the emotions you're experiencing. This will bring clarity to your situation and help you release a lot of the anger, sadness and grief you are feeling.

It's nice during a sad time to have someone take care of you and make you feel momentarily better. Get a relaxing massage to release both the emotional and physical toxins from your body, pet your dog or ask a friend for a good hug. You could probably use lots of them.

Head out with a friend to your favorite restaurant and over lunch or dinner process the relationship and the breakup. You'll feel loved and supported by someone who really cares about you.

Make or buy your favorite comfort food. Whether it's macaroni and cheese or a certain cookie your mom used to make, it will *momentarily* take you back to warm and fuzzier times.

Watch old TV shows or movies that make you laugh. You know what they say, laughter is the best medicine. I always love *I Love Lucy* reruns to cheer me up.

If you are up to it, volunteer somewhere or offer to assist a friend with a project. Helping others makes you feel better and takes your mind off your own troubles for a bit.

Everything can feel really blue after a breakup so consider starting a "Gratitude Journal" to remind yourself of three wonderful things you are grateful for each and every day, even if it's *the sky is a beautiful blue* or *my dog loves me*. It's going to keep you grounded and it will help you counter some of the sadness that can be overwhelming you right now.

Give yourself the gift of grieving and mourning the end of the relationship. Don't hold back. Let the tears flow. It's healthy, it's a release and it will ultimately help you heal.

Should the sadness get too heavy, get help from a counselor or a trusted friend to help you cope.

Most importantly, wait to date until you've healed. It's tempting to substitute one man for another but it rarely works. When you don't take the time you need to reflect and heal before dating again, you end up bringing your open wounds (also known as baggage) into a new relationship.

You'll know when the time is right to date again. You'll be able to tell because you'll no longer feel the intense emotions of anger or sadness you're feeling now when you think about him.

See this period in your life as an exciting time to discover yourself again. When you've been with someone for a while, it's hard to imagine creating a single life again. Realizing who you are again can be exciting and a lot of fun while you're going through the healing process.

Try signing up for classes you've always wanted to take or go see a fun chick flick by yourself or with a friend. In most cities MeetUp.com groups offer tons of fun activities. Get up the courage to try one out. You'll get to meet new like-minded friends who love doing what you like to do.

Breakups are hard. When you can see them as an opportunity to get some clarity and to heal, you will find that new doors start opening again fairly quickly. All you have to do is be willing to open the new door when you're ready. Then walk through and discover the magic waiting for you on the other side.

12 Dating Resolutions To Live By

"We're all a little weird. And life is a little weird. And when we find someone whose weirdness is compatible with ours, we join up with them and fall into mutually satisfying weirdness – and call it love – true love!" ~Unshakeablebelief.com

Resolution #1

Start on your new dating journey by treating yourself to a makeover – maybe a new haircut, a shift in hair color, a new lipstick or a fun dating outfit. You'll feel better, look better and you'll stoke the fire of your inner glow that men are so attracted to.

Resolution #2

Come up with a Dating Blueprint that's going to help you figure out where you'll find the types of men you're looking for.

Resolution #3

Go on a date with the intention of having fun – nothing more – see where it takes you.

It will eliminate the pressure for having to figure out if he's "the one" in the first 15 minutes. Snap decisions about a man can lead you to miss a good guy!

Resolution #4

Rediscover your flirting skills. Smile and talk with men everywhere you go. You want to get comfortable interacting with men and this takes practice, practice, and more practice!

Resolution #5

Men are visual creatures. They are initially attracted to you on a sexual level and it's true: given half a chance, they will try their best to have sex with you ASAP.

Instead of being turned off by a man's advances, understand this is his way of letting you know he's into you!

FYI: it's okay to set sexual boundaries and the time to have sex is when YOU – not the guy – is ready.

Resolution #6

Instead of telling yourself, "I love who I am but," work on accepting yourself as the "one of a kind, magnificent, lovable woman you truly are!"

Resolution #7

Give a nice man a chance. Sometimes it can take three or four dates for the chemistry to click between the two of you. And a man who might not be so cute on date number one, can seem like Richard Gere by date number four once you've gotten to know his personality.

Resolution #8

In the next few months, find at least three activities you would love to try. This brings out your inner passion and stokes the inner glow that makes you feel sexy, something men are really attracted to.

New activities give you something fun to do versus sitting around thinking about men. You just might meet a great guy or you might make a new friend you have something in common with.

Resolution #9

Get a really clear vision of the type of man you want! Consider dating someone slightly different than the men of your past. They didn't work for some reason but a new type just might.

Resolution #10

Periodically remove your profile from a dating site for a day or two. You'll be considered "new" when you go back on. Guess who gets noticed first by men on the site...the women who are "new" to the site.

Resolution #11

Don't quit or give up on dating! If you do, you will be right where you are today, hoping and dreaming about a great man versus having a real one you can share your life with.

Resolution #12

If you find yourself having a really hard time with dating, consider investing in yourself and your dating life by coaching with me one-on-one. I can give you the short cuts for finding Quality Men and I'd love to share secrets for dating that are geared to you and your specific issues.

I offer a Complimentary Find Your Soul Mate Discovery Session where we can talk about the dating issues you're facing and whether we are a good fit to work together. You can contact me at **Lisa@findaqualityman.com.**

I hope you've enjoyed discovering *The Winning Dating*

Formula For Women Over 50. Keep this book close by. It's a great reference you can refer back to over and over again for help with your dating journey.

If you have questions or comments, I'd love to hear them. You can write to me at **Lisa@FindAQualityMan.com**.

You have lots of choices when it comes to relationships at this time in your life. Enjoy meeting lots of new men, whether they are datable or not. It's important to get yourself around male energy as much as you can. It's great practice and you know what they say, "Practice makes perfect."

Go use what you've learned and start having fun dating lots of great men! I'm here for you as your mentor on this exciting journey.

To Your Dating Success!

Lots of hugs to you~

Lisa

PS. Want to learn more? Sign up for my free report, *5 Little Known Secrets To Finding A Quality Man*, at **www.FindAQualityMan.com**.

Are you ready to meet YOUR MR. RIGHT?

If so, let's set up a complimentary 30-minute session where you and I can talk about what's going on in your dating life. During our conversation, I'll give you a plan with some tips you can go out and use right away to attract your Mr. Right.

To reserve your spot, send an email to Lisa@findaqualityman.com. Then keep an eye on your inbox because I'll send you a link to my calendar to set up our time to talk.

Made in the USA
Monee, IL
28 October 2020